Gallery Books
Editor: Peter Fallon

BLACKWATER ANGEL

Jim Nolan

BLACKWATER ANGEL

Gallery Books

Blackwater Angel
is first published
simultaneously in paperback
and in a clothbound edition
on the day of its première,
8 May 2001.

The Gallery Press
Loughcrew
Oldcastle
County Meath
Ireland

© Jim Nolan 2001

ISBN 1 85235 285 x (*paperback*)
    1 85235 286 8 (*clothbound*)

All rights whatsoever in this play are strictly reserved. Requests to reproduce the text in whole or in part, and application for performance in any medium, by professional or amateur companies, or for translation into any language should be addressed to the publishers.
    The Gallery Press acknowledges the financial assistance of An Chomhairle Ealaíon / The Arts Council, Ireland, and the Arts Council of Northern Ireland.

Characters

VALENTINE GREATRAKES, *a healer*
RUTH GODOLPHIN, *Greatrakes' wife*
LIZZIE MAHER, *servant*
MICHAEL MAHER, *servant*
THOMAS WYVERN, *manservant*
MATHIAS EVERARD, *actor manager*
EUSTACIA EVERARD, *his wife, an actress*
ANGEL LANDY, *singer*
MARTIN REILLY, *a blind man*
ELLEN REILLY, *his wife*

Travelling players, servants, a young boy.

Time and place

The play is set in the interior of Valentine Greatrakes' castle, and in a nearby forest, at Affane, County Waterford, in the summer of 1666.

Blackwater Angel was first produced in the Abbey Theatre, Dublin, on Tuesday, 8 May 2001, with the following cast:

GREATRAKES	John Lynch
RUTH	Julia Lane
LIZZIE MAHER	Catherine Walsh
MICHAEL MAHER	Michael Hayes
THOMAS WYVERN	Chris McHallem
EVERARD	Robert O'Mahoney
EUSTACIA	Cathy White
ANGEL LANDY	Laura Rogers
ELLEN REILLY	Gertrude Montgomery
MARTIN REILLY	Conan Sweeny
THEATRICAL TROUPE AND OTHER ROLES	Lise Hearns
	Gertude Montgomery
	Conan Sweeny
	Jude Sweeney

Director	Ben Barnes
Set Design	Jamie Vartan
Costume Design	Joan O'Clery
Lighting	Rupert Murray
Composer	Ilona Sekacz
Stage Director	Finola Eustace
Assistant Director	David Parnell
ASMs	Stephen Dempsey, Gabby McGrath

for Trudi and Megan

PROLOGUE

As the pre-set fades to black we hear a disembodied voice proclaim:

The great cures and strange miracles performed by Mr Valentine Greatrakes, who restoreth the blind to sight, the deaf to hearing, the lame to strength — and cripples to walk without crutches. It being a time of great expectation among all men, and of strange impressions upon very many . . . it is no wonder, when all men look for a year of miracles, that one man should attempt to begin it.

As the last word is heard, the double doors of Greatrakes' castle swing violently open and a shaft of white light invades the interior. GREATRAKES *stands alone in the open doorway. A single bass drumbeat is heard, followed by two more in rapid succession. The drumbeat continues in this rhythm and gradually increases in intensity as* GREATRAKES *comes forward. His attention is focussed firmly on the* YOUNG BOY *who has entered the theatre and approaches him tentatively through the central aisle of the auditorium. Barefoot and poorly dressed, the boy's face is grotesquely deformed, his eyes, cheeks and throat covered in a mass of putrid open sores.*

GREATRAKES (*As the* BOY *joins him onstage and the drumbeat ceases*) Do not be afraid.
BOY I'm afeard of nothin', sir.
GREATRAKES I am glad to hear it. What is your name?
BOY Michael, sir.
GREATRAKES Is that all?
BOY Michael Maher, sir.
GREATRAKES From which parish, Michael?
BOY From Salterbridge, sir. The parish of Lismore. I have travelled far.
GREATRAKES Let us hope the journey will prove worthwhile.

BOY   Do you know why you are here, Michael?
BOY   To be cured, sir.
GREATRAKES   And do you think you will be?
BOY   I'm not countin' on it, sir.
GREATRAKES   (*Smiling*) Wise man. We shall see, Michael. (GREATRAKES *lays his hands on the boy's face, stroking in turn his eyes, cheeks and throat as he intones with increasing intensity*) May God Almighty heal thee for His mercy's sake. May God Almighty heal thee for His mercy's sake. May God Almighty heal thee for His mercy's sake. (*Pause*) Go now.

The BOY *goes. Stops. Turns.*

BOY   Except the dark, Mr Greatrakes.
GREATRAKES   What about it?
BOY   I'm afeard of nothin', sir — except the dark.

The BOY *leaves.* GREATRAKES *watches him go.*

GREATRAKES   And so we waited. (*Pause*) Afterwards, the boy told me how on that long journey home, crossing the Blackwater on the footbridge at Cappoquin, he encountered a party of youths returning from the Free School at Lismore. As they passed him, they stopped to mock and jeer at his pockmarked face, at the hideous swelling which covered his eyes and threatened to blind him, at the putrid sores which ringed his throat, the rancid odour emanating from the open wounds in his hands. How in his own parish, the boundaries of which he had never crossed until that morning, none had ever suffered to abuse him thus. This was so, he said, because in his own place, it was understood that his deformity atoned for the sins of the parish as well as his own. As the youths taunted him across the span of the footbridge, the boy knew for the first time that such wisdom did not prevail in the great world beyond his own fields. He told me how, as dusk fell and nearing home, his mouth parched from the dry, dusty road he had travelled, he stopped to drink from the well of St Carthage. And, as he knelt to quench his thirst, how in the fading evening light he encountered his reflection in the well and saw, for the first time, the nature and scale of his deformity. How, at that instant, it was no longer the dark which frightened him. How, at that instant also, he *was* now counting on me. (*Pause*) And so we waited, the child in hope and I — the instrument of that hope — in naked terror. Because he was the first — and after him there would be no going back. (*Pause*) Three days later the boy returned, his swollen eyes abated, his throat strangely amended, the festering sores on his cheeks and hands now closed and dry. 'I have come to thank you for your trouble,' he said. And whatever way he said that word and whatever way those new-minted eyes looked into mine as he spoke, he knew and I knew, assuredly, that trouble is what it would bring. That evening they lit bonfires in Salterbridge. The boy's father bore him on his shoulder from one end of the village to the other and the people of that parish gave thanks to God. For they knew that the great burden the boy had borne for them had been lifted and they knew that the sins of the village had been atoned for. (*Pause*) In the darkness of this house I knew something also: that the Holy One of Israel, among so many more pious, more wise and more learned, had made choice of so poor and so vile and so contemptible a wretch as I to be an instrument of His mercy and deliverance to afflicted poor creatures. *I had been chosen.* But I did not know why. All I did know was that even as the maimed and diseased and the scarred were already clamouring at the gate for my touch, a price would one day be exacted for a gift I had neither sought or desired but which was now irrevocably mine.

Lights fade on GREATRAKES *and come up instantly on Scene One.*

ACT ONE

Scene One

Greatrakes' castle. Late afternoon. As lights come up, LIZZIE, *Greatrakes' servant girl, is setting two places at either end of a long oak table.* RUTH, *Greatrakes' wife, enters from another room.*

RUTH   Nothing?
LIZZIE   Nothing yet, Ma'am.
RUTH   There are few things on which my husband can be depended, Lizzie. Tardiness, it seems, is still one of them. (*Pause*) Has Thomas returned?
LIZZIE   No, Ma'am.
RUTH   Then we live in hope! Poor Thomas! I'll warrant they'll appoint him Master of the Youghal Harbour if he spends another day languishing at that infernal dockside.
LIZZIE   I'm sure the Master will come today, Ma'am.
RUTH   How do I look?
LIZZIE   (*Without enthusiasm*) Very becoming, Ma'am.
RUTH   Not that Mr Greatrakes will notice, but after six months *someone* should make the effort.
LIZZIE   The dress is lovely, Ma'am.
RUTH   Mother's castoffs, Lizzie. She sent over a box full when — well, you know when.
LIZZIE   Have you heard from the children?
RUTH   Father wrote. 'Boys thriving, little Mary less so, but will catch up. Cornwall air most agreeable to their complexions — you should try it. Most affectionate pater, Sir William Godolphin, Baronet.' Goodness, Lizzie, no one save my father can make the contents of a letter sound like a medical report and his signature like the billhead of an Act of

Parliament!
LIZZIE He means well, I suppose.
RUTH He *means* never to forgive me for marrying a Cromwellian soldier. Not to mention one who discovers he can heal the sick, draws every cripple in Ireland to his gate, and then disappears to England at the whim of some migrainous Lady Something-or-other, leaving us to clean up in his absence. (*Pause*) Am I being unfair?
LIZZIE That's not for me to say, Ma'am.
RUTH You're all so infuriatingly loyal to him, aren't you?
LIZZIE I believe you are too, Ma'am.
RUTH Indeed! At least tell me I did right to send the children away.
LIZZIE They're as well out of this madness, Ma'am — and that's for sure.
RUTH I trust Mr Greatrakes will be of like mind when he hears.
LIZZIE It won't be for long, Ma'am. You'll see — you'll have them back in no time.
RUTH I hope so. He must attend to those poor unfortunates the moment he returns. Then, soon perhaps, we can all get back to an *acceptable* degree of upheaval.

MICHAEL *enters.*

MICHAEL (*To* RUTH) The cripples is fed and watered, Ma'am.
RUTH Michael, how many times must I tell you? Those are human beings in that yard — not horses.
MICHAEL I'm well aware of it, Ma'am — for there's no room for the horses. The cripples has commandeered the last of the stalls in the stables beyond.
RUTH How many more today?
MICHAEL A baker's dozen, Ma'am — unlucky for some. Though 'tis more than luck some of them boys will need. There's an oul' lad over from Wexford way, Lizzie, that has the fits of the falling on him.

Six days, they say, traipsin' the roads to get here. I'll warrant if he falls again he'll not get up. (*To* RUTH) And more that has the weepin' leprosies, Ma'am. (*To* LIZZIE) They're beyond in the malt-house if you fancied to see them.

LIZZIE I *have* seen them.

MICHAEL The plague of London has nothin' on what's in that yard. And each day addin' to the misery of the one before. It's the wonder of God we're not all infected, Ma'am.

RUTH Yes, Michael, it *is* the wonder of God. We would do well to remember it. How stands Affane, Lizzie?

LIZZIE Burstin' at the seams, Ma'am. The gateman at the hostel there did tell me three more arrives for every one tires waitin' for him.

MICHAEL There must be two thousand waitin' for the cure, Ma'am.

RUTH I see. (*Pause*) Well, Mr Greatrakes will be busy then, won't he?

MICHAEL Something else, Ma'am. Thomas and me have been feeding the cripples as you instructed.

RUTH It's the least we can do, is it not?

MICHAEL It is, Ma'am — so long as there's something to feed them. The wheat loft is near empty. At the rate they're devouring it, there'll be no bread in two days.

RUTH Then Thomas must go to the merchant in Lismore. Our credit is good, is it not?

LIZZIE Thomas has been going to the merchant for over a month now, Ma'am. Your credit has run out.

MICHAEL Jackson says he'll supply the needs of the house until the Master's return. But, to quote himself, (*Accent*) 'I'll not stand exposed to an army of lepers!'

RUTH Christ will never be forgotten whilst Mr Jackson endures. (*Pause*) Well, then we must hope that Mr Greatrakes will bring a heavy purse along with his healing touch.

A trapdoor concealed in the floor opens suddenly and with some violence. VALENTINE GREATRAKES *ascends with a flourish.*

GREATRAKES Ask and you shall receive! Your most humble servant, Madam — late but not, I trust, lamented!

He embraces RUTH.

RUTH (*Shocked and delighted but trying not to show it*) Mr Greatrakes. The manner of your return is no less sudden than your leavetaking.

GREATRAKES Predictability, Madam, is the chief enemy of a good marriage.

RUTH Then ours must be in very good order. For you are nothing if not a constant surprise.

GREATRAKES I shall take that as a compliment. (*Kisses her*) I have missed you, Ruth.

RUTH (*Bashful in front of* LIZZIE *and* MICHAEL *whom* GREATRAKES *has not seen*) Yes. And Lizzie and Michael too, I dare say.

GREATRAKES (*Notices them for the first time*) Mea culpa! The good and faithful servants!

LIZZIE You're welcome home, Master.

GREATRAKES I thank you for it, Lizzie. (*Suddenly remembers* THOMAS) Dear Lord! Thomas! I'd quite forgotten.

Opens trapdoor.

Are you there, Thomas?

THOMAS (*From below, as a travelling bag is hurtled up through the door*) I am here, sir. (*As he appears laden with other bags*) If just about!

THOMAS *is now onstage. We see that he walks with a pronounced limp.*

Your service, Madam. And my apologies for the circumspect entrance.

RUTH Yes. We had rather anticipated the front door.
GREATRAKES That was my fault. Thomas informed me of the welcoming party at the gates. We hired a cot at Youghal and came by the Blackwater. Did you know, Ruth, there's a tunnel runs all the way from the basement to the riverbank?
RUTH I was not acquainted with it.
GREATRAKES Apparently my grandfather had it dug, the time of the first plantation. Designed for a hasty retreat from marauding natives, I'll warrant, but we were glad of it today, were we not, Thomas?
THOMAS You were, sir.
RUTH The Master will eat now, Lizzie. (*Slightly barbed*) I'm sure he must be hungry after his long journey.
LIZZIE Yes, Ma'am.

LIZZIE *exits.*

THOMAS If there's nothing else, sir, I'll take your bags to your chamber.

THOMAS *exits.*

MICHAEL What will I tell the cripples, Master?
GREATRAKES (*Testily*) Tell them nothing.
MICHAEL But they're waitin' for the curin'.
GREATRAKES (*As* LIZZIE *returns*) Then let them wait. I am tired, boy! I have been aboard ship these three days from Bristol. Before that, two days on horseback from my Lady Conway's in Warwickshire. And before that since, three days by carriage from London. Now, does that not entitle me to the comforts of my own house, without my servant boy dare to play my conscience?
MICHAEL I am sorry, sir, but I did not bid them come.
GREATRAKES And I did! (MICHAEL *does not reply*) Yes. I did, didn't I? Because after you, there was no going back. (*Pause*) Perhaps I ought to have left you as I found you, Michael.

MICHAEL   That's as maybe now, Master. You did not.

> MICHAEL *exits. Silence.* LIZZIE, *who has witnessed this exchange, begins to serve food at the table.*

RUTH   *(Finally)* So . . . You returned by way of Warwickshire.
GREATRAKES   Yes. I did. *(Without rancour)* And I may, may I not?
RUTH   How is your Lady Conway?
GREATRAKES   She continues poorly. I thought to try to heal her one last time on my way from London.
RUTH   I have waited five months, Valentine. I imagine you must have thought five days more a small trifle.
GREATRAKES   I had no means to inform you.
RUTH   It is Thomas who would have been grateful for news. He is quite exhausted.
GREATRAKES   Then we have much in common. For I am exhausted too.
RUTH   I regret to hear it. *(Pause)* Thank you, Lizzie.

> LIZZIE *exits.*

GREATRAKES   She is one of the most remarkable women of her time, Ruth. She is versed in Latin, Greek and Theology and can discourse on Astronomy and Alchemy as well as any man.
RUTH   That is fine testimony, sir.
GREATRAKES   Yes, it is! Entirely self taught too. She had to be. No school would take her, you see. Because for every day of her thirty-four years she has been grievously troubled by headaches so violent as do hurl her entire body into paroxysm. Yet for all she endures, she refuses to be slave to her suffering.
RUTH   Indeed!
GREATRAKES   She is liked and admired by some of England's finest minds. And do you know why, Ruth?

	Because she is a good woman. And they, like I, feel privileged to know her.
RUTH	I would you should speak so highly of any that line the road to Affane or huddle for shelter in the malthouse, these five months past.
GREATRAKES	I do not wish to speak of Affane! I wish to speak of what I have witnessed, Ruth! There is a world beyond these fields, you know.
RUTH	Yes. I remember it.
GREATRAKES	And I have seen it! Do you know where I have been, Ruth? Do you know what I have borne witness to?
RUTH	You have just told me. I am deeply moved.
GREATRAKES	She is a good woman. Is it not allowed it should trouble me God sent me to heal her and I failed?
RUTH	One hundred and fifty-five pounds sent you.
GREATRAKES	How dare you!
RUTH	God had plenty to engage you here, Valentine, amongst those who had nothing to pay.
GREATRAKES	You know I never sought or received a penny from any I healed here. That money was compensation only — left here with you to run my estate in my absence.
RUTH	It is gone, Valentine. Every penny of it. Used to feed those who waited here for you in vain.
GREATRAKES	I could not be in two places!
RUTH	Then you should have stayed here.
GREATRAKES	I went where God desired me!
RUTH	Why, then, is God in Lady Conway's pocket also?
GREATRAKES	That's enough!
RUTH	Yes it is.

She moves towards exit.

You should eat. You will need your strength. There are near two thousand await your touch.

GREATRAKES I find I am no longer hungry.
RUTH Then rest. I will tell them you are home and will start tomorrow.

GREATRAKES You will tell them nothing until I bid you. (*Pause.* RUTH *begins to leave*) I believe it were God's design, Ruth. I did not ask to go to England. I did not ask for any of this. You say two thousand. I touched five times that number in Lincoln's Inn Field. When my rooms in Gray's Inn became known the courtyard was thronged day and night, not just by hundreds who beseeched a cure but by as many more who came to stare in wonder and as many again who came to ridicule, thinking me some charlatan or mountebank. The Attorney General of England says that I have made the greatest disturbance between clergy and laymen that any have ever seen. I did not tell you in my letters because I thought not to frighten you but I was summoned by the King himself to account for my actions.

RUTH Why should it trouble the King you heal his subjects?

GREATRAKES Because curing the King's Evil is the prerogative of kings, evidence of their divine right to rule. King Charles is not so comfortable on his throne as would please him have a former Cromwellian soldier compete with him for miracles.

RUTH Is that what you think they are?

GREATRAKES I do not know. I have never known. I believe the hand of God is in my hand but know not if that makes for miracle. This I do know, however: it is a question the best minds in England are now asking in my wake.

RUTH Then let them ask. Those who await your touch care not for its source.

GREATRAKES But I must.

RUTH Why must you?

GREATRAKES Because I am frightened. These are dangerous times, Ruth. The world is rational and wonders have ceased. There is no trust in anything that cannot be by some law accounted for. Our church says only the Papists require trickery, that no pretence of miracle is to be hearkened to when the doctrine we are to believe in is already established.

RUTH　Then do not heed the church.

GREATRAKES　I must.

RUTH　Why? You did not heed them three years ago.

GREATRAKES　That was different.

RUTH　Was it? The Dean of Lismore forbid you to practise because you did not have his silly licence. You said you knew of no law of God or nation which prohibited any person from doing what good he could for his neighbour. What is so different now?

GREATRAKES　There is a village in Warwickshire goes by the name of Husband's Bosworth. I passed through it once. The apple blossoms were in bloom on the high street, children were playing in the village square. Three weeks ago in that same square, nine white witches were executed for curing the falling sickness. I am frightened, Ruth.

RUTH　You are no witch!

GREATRAKES　They know not what I am! I have friends in important places, true. Many who have sworn good testimony to my integrity. But there *are* others, Ruth. Who take me for impostor. Who take me for conjuror. And one who published a pamphlet wherein he accuses me of sedition.

RUTH　Sedition! How so?

GREATRAKES　That in curing the King's Evil, I would level the King's gift as, in Cromwell's army, I once sought to level his office. With a design that, when it appeared the King could *do* no more than other men, he should *be* no more than others. If the King should believe as much, Ruth —

RUTH　The King is not an idiot, whatever about your pamphleteer.

GREATRAKES　Would you stake my life on it? It is the temperature of the times. Neither theology nor politics has room for what I peddle.

RUTH You do not *peddle* anything! Your hands are touched by the hand of God. Let your philosophers and pamphleteers make of that what they will. God will protect you.

GREATRAKES Will He protect me from myself? (*Pause*) I did not ask for any of this.

RUTH I know that. But it is yours. Come to bed, Valentine. Sleep in my arms tonight — I will give you peace.

GREATRAKES (*Embrace. Sudden panic*) Ruth, where are the children? I had forgotten the children. (*She does not reply*) Where are they, Ruth?

RUTH They are safe.

GREATRAKES Where are they!

RUTH The multitude frightened them.

GREATRAKES Damn the multitude! I am heartily sick of the multitude! Where are my children!

RUTH They would run in terror from the diseased. I sent them to my father's house in Cornwall for safekeeping.

GREATRAKES You had no right to send them away without my permission.

RUTH You were not here to give permission. I did as I saw fit. They will return as soon as the crowds abate.

GREATRAKES And when, pray tell, will that be?

RUTH When you have done as God ordains you must do.

Lights fade. End of Scene One.

Scene Two

Greatrakes' castle. Some days later. LIZZIE *alone on stage, engaged in some domestic activity or other.* MICHAEL *enters.*

LIZZIE   You're back.

MICHAEL   No, 'tis me shadow only. Myself is beyond in Youghal still, quaffing tankards in the Widow Shanahan's tavern. (*Taking off boots*) Is there anythin' to drink — the dust on that road has me tongue scalded.

LIZZIE   If not silenced. (*Pouring him some cider*) I'm worse to be concerned for ye.

MICHAEL   Y'are too. For if 'twas me mother and not my sister you were intended, I'm sure God would have designed it that way. (*She gives him drink*)

LIZZIE   I didn't hear the horses in the yard.

MICHAEL   No, because there's no room for them, remember. I've stabled them at Osborne's place for the duration. Is there any stir on himself?

LIZZIE   Not yet.

MICHAEL   Fit for him to be reposin' these six days on the bed above. It must have been more than strokin' cripples he was beyond in London.

LIZZIE   Mind your place, Michael.

MICHAEL   I will, alright. And tell me, sister, is it my place to have the shirt near ripped from me back be the cripples on the road from Osborne's? (*Gestures to shirt*) Look! They know he's back, Lizzie. And they want to know when he's comin' out.

LIZZIE   When he's good and ready, I'll warrant.

MICHAEL   Well I do wish he'd let *them* know when that great day is going to come. Because if he does not, they'll bate down that door beyond and come lookin' for him and I do not want to be around when that happens.

LIZZIE   Nothing's going to happen. The Master is tired, is all. He'll attend to the crowds when he's fit and

able.
MICHAEL You think he can do no wrong, don't you, Lizzie?
LIZZIE He did no wrong by you. You should remember that. And as for thinkin' — I'm seldom inclined to it. You should do the same.
MICHAEL I will. When I'm old and grey and have given up on the world. In the meantime, I do like *two* sleeves to my shirt.
LIZZIE (*Laughs*) Give it to me so. I'll stitch it for ye — and yer lip with it.
MICHAEL (*Gives her his shirt*) You might wash and starch it while you're at it.
LIZZIE What are you wantin' with a starched shirt?
MICHAEL 'Tis for the playactin'.
LIZZIE What playactin'?
MICHAEL There's an English crowd pitchin' a tent at the edge of the wood — I passed them on the way home. (*Bows*) Madam Eustacia and Mr Mathias Everard's Celebrated Theatre of Delights!
LIZZIE Sounds like just the medicine for this place.
MICHAEL The cripples must have drawn them on us. Though God love the playactors, they'll not make their fortune from those boyos. Unless they're to pay in boils and tumours.
LIZZIE Michael!
MICHAEL Did you ever see a play, Lizzie?
LIZZIE I did not. I thought that class of thing was banned from city and country.
MICHAEL Ah that was in oul' Cromwell's time. They say the King beyond in London now does be very fond of them. You might come with me, Lizzie.
LIZZIE I might not. There's enough drama going on around here without I should go to a tent to pay for it.
MICHAEL Well I'm for it, anyway. Take good sight of me now when you can, Lizzie. (*Leaps onto chair in dramatic pose.* RUTH *enters.* LIZZIE, *but not* MICHAEL, *sees her*) For who knows, with my starched shirt and my devilish good looks, maybe Madam

	Eustacia might sign me up and I'll be away out of this hellhole — never more to return! (*Notices* RUTH) Ah, Mistress Greatrakes. (*Down from chair. Scrambles for shirt*) I didn't hear you coming in.
RUTH	Clearly not. And who, pray tell, is Madam Eustacia?
MICHAEL	One of the English playactors has arrived in the village below, Ma'am.
RUTH	I see. And the lucky woman is going to spirit you away from this 'hellhole', is she?
LIZZIE	It was just a bit of levity, Ma'am. He meant no harm.
MICHAEL	That's right, Ma'am — I was only sportin'.
RUTH	I'm relieved to hear it, Michael! But just in case you do disappear, now that Mr Greatrakes has returned we have settled our accounts with that exemplar of Christian charity, Mr 'Army of Lepers' Jackson. He stands presently in the yard with a delivery of flour. You might help him unload it, Michael.
MICHAEL	Yes, Ma'am.
RUTH	(*A smile to* LIZZIE) One hundred and thirty bags, I believe.
MICHAEL	(*Between his teeth*) 'Twill be a pleasure, Ma'am.

MICHAEL *nods to* RUTH *before scurrying out.*

RUTH	Playactors, eh? A timely diversion, Lizzie.
LIZZIE	I should think it will take more than plays to divert them poor unfortunates, Ma'am.
RUTH	For us, I mean. It might be just what we need.
LIZZIE	Do you think so, Ma'am?

GREATRAKES *enters. He carries a leather writing satchel and a pair of riding boots.*

	Would you care to eat, sir?
GREATRAKES	(*Puts satchel on table. Sits. Puts boots on*) Thank you, Lizzie, but there are more pressing matters at hand. Fetch Thomas for me, would you?

LIZZIE Yes, sir.

        LIZZIE *exits.*

RUTH You are rested, I hope.
GREATRAKES Not rested, Ruth. But resolved.
RUTH I am glad to hear it. (*Tentatively*) And so, going out, I see.

        Pause.

GREATRAKES Yes.
RUTH God be praised!

        She begins to leave.

I shall let them know in the yard. Those in the barn have been here longest — we must start with them.
GREATRAKES Ruth! (*He stops her*) I am not going to the yard. Not today.
RUTH But you said —
GREATRAKES I said I was going out.
RUTH *Then where else is there to go?*
GREATRAKES I have important business —
RUTH Your 'business' is outside that door, Valentine. If you could but see what those poor wretches endure, you would fly to their aid. And you must!
GREATRAKES You think I don't know what they endure?
RUTH I think you have forgotten it. You have lain six days between clean sheets; there are children in that barn who have been lying as many weeks in their own waste.
GREATRAKES I have not been idle! I slept not more than six hours in those six days.
RUTH What, does your conscience trouble you?
GREATRAKES *You* are not my conscience.
RUTH Then look to it yourself — if you can find it.

GREATRAKES   I know where it resides. And I'll trouble you not to wrestle with it. (*Pause*) I have taken steps, Ruth.
RUTH   What steps? It is no more than thirty across that yard — to where you are needed.
GREATRAKES   And I will take them — when I am able!
RUTH   When will that be, Valentine? Tomorrow? Or the next day? Or the next thereafter? You have promised as much every day since you returned. Must you wait until someone dies?

> THOMAS *enters. He is followed by* MICHAEL *and* LIZZIE.

THOMAS   Then he need wait no longer, Mistress.
MICHAEL   The old lad from over Wexford way, Ma'am. The one with the falling sickness.
THOMAS   He will fall no more, sir.

> *Silence.*

GREATRAKES   I must wait until I am able — even if a hundred should die. None of you are my conscience. Look on me whatever way you will but you are *not* my conscience. (*Pause. To* THOMAS) Go by way of the tunnel to the riverbank. Stand to with the cot. I will join you presently. (*To* MICHAEL) You, have the body removed from the yard this instant. (*To* LIZZIE) Lizzie, go to the Minister. (*A glance to* RUTH) Make arrangements for a burial.

> THOMAS *exits through the trapdoor.* LIZZIE *and* MICHAEL *exit.* RUTH *kneels and prays in silence.*

I am not a monster, Ruth. (*Pause.* RUTH *looks at him*) Seek you my tears as proof? (*Gestures to eyes*) Then have them! Catch them in a pail and bring them to the barn and lay them down beside that man's body. Take my heart with it. Carve it up

	and divide it amongst them. Let them see that Greatrakes has tears too, that he has suffered also!
RUTH	I do not doubt it, Valentine. I know you are troubled.
GREATRAKES	And do you know that I am a good man? Not without blemish, but a good man withal?
RUTH	You do not need to ask.
GREATRAKES	I believe I do. I think you doubt it now. But I have testimony, Ruth. Not just for you, but for the world. (*Pulls sheaves of paper from satchel*) I have not been idle, see. I have matched their pamphlets with my own. I have returned good for evil. Look you, see! Testimonials! Over seventy of them. Listen to this —
RUTH	I do not need to.
GREATRAKES	Listen, I say! 'He appears to me of too open a disposition to be able to conceal and disguise himself. He is void of all covetousness, pride and hatred of others. His charity and goodwill to mankind seem to be great and to be the only thing which moves him to engage himself in such perpetual labours.' Simon Patrick, Rector of St Paul's Church, Covent Garden, April Fourteenth, 1666.
RUTH	Valentine —
GREATRAKES	Here's another from the poet, Andrew Marvell: 'Mr Greatrakes is a man of free, generous and open spirit without anything of affectation or reservedness, of singular patience and tender-heartedness towards all persons in pain or trouble.' Mark you, Ruth! Testimony. To my good name!
RUTH	I have no need of testimony on that account.
GREATRAKES	No? There are dozens like it. All from men of good position and authority. And dozens more who lay testimony to the work I have carried out in God's name. It is all here, Ruth. I have set it all down so the world will know. That is no monster they describe. That is no ogre whose good name

and works they testify to. That is your husband, Ruth.

RUTH   I know it, Valentine. Do you?

Silence.

GREATRAKES   No. (*Pause*) No. Because I doubt it now, also.

He returns sheaves of paper to satchel and goes to trapdoor.

RUTH   Where are you to?
GREATRAKES   To Sir Richard Boyle's at Lismore. He sails tomorrow for London. I mean he should bring these to his son Robert who has vowed to have them published.
RUTH   And then?
GREATRAKES   I do not know. You think this 'gift' — the very word mocks me — can be drawn like water from the village standpipe. Well, you must learn, as I have, that it cannot. For I am *not* some mountebank or conjuror — it is *not* a trick. (*Pause*) I am weary, Ruth. I should have listened to you. When I first had this impulse and confided it to you, do you remember what you said?
RUTH   I ascribed it to some strange imagination. (*Pause*) And bid you keep your silence on it.
GREATRAKES   Would that I had, Ruth. Was it just vanity prevented me?
RUTH   Whatever your failings, Valentine, vanity is not one of them.
GREATRAKES   I *was* seduced though. To have been chosen. I never told you, Ruth. The first time. When I healed Michael. There was a moment — a precise moment when I knew it would work. And at that moment — though, God forgive me, it may be blasphemy to say it — the blood of Christ it was and not my own was coursing through my veins. It were akin to ecstasy. (*Pause*) You knew what

	that would cost, didn't you?
RUTH	You cannot go back, Valentine. You own it now and must pay the price.
GREATRAKES	Whatever it may amount to?
RUTH	You have no choice. I will address the crowds. I will tell them you are ill-disposed. (*Pause*) And that you will go to them when — as you said — you are able.

GREATRAKES *begins to descend through the trapdoor.*

Valentine. (*He stops*) I know that you are a good man.

GREATRAKES *closes the trapdoor.* RUTH *leaves to address the crowds. Lights fade.*

Scene Three

A theatre stage, later that evening. We open on what transpires to be a rehearsal of the final scene of John Ford's The Broken Heart. *The part of* CALANTHA *is played by* EUSTACIA EVERARD, *that of* NEARCHUS *by* MATHIAS EVERARD, *and the other parts by members of the theatrical troupe. The scene concludes as follows:*

CALANTHA One kiss on these cold lips, my last! *(Kisses* ITHOCLES*)* Argos now's Sparta's king. Command the voice
Which waits now, to sing the song I fitted for my end.
BASSANES Her 'heart is broken' indeed. Oh royal maid, 'would thou hadst missed this part! Yet 'twas a brave one. I must weep to see her smile in death.
ARMOSTES Wise Tecnicus! Thus said he:
'When youth is ripe, and age from time doth part. The lifeless trunk shall wed the Broken Heart. 'Tis here fulfilled.
NEARCHUS I am your king.
ALL Long live Nearchus, King of Sparta!
NEARCHUS Her last will
Shall never be digressed from; wait in order
Upon these faithful lovers, as becomes us.
The councils of the Gods are never known,
Till men can call the effects of them their own.

> *Applause.* GREATRAKES *comes forward from the back of the auditorium, emerging along the centre aisle. We are to understand that he has been covertly watching the rehearsal from the back of the 'tent'.*

GREATRAKES Bravo! Bravo! Felicitations, one and all!
EVERARD Who goes there?
GREATRAKES Your humble servant, sir. That was stirring stuff.
EVERARD *That* was a rehearsal, sir — we open tomorrow night. If you're one of the Lord Lieutenant's men,

33

GREATRAKES (*As he reaches the stage*) I am nobody's man, sir, save God's.
EVERARD We have no truck with Ministers. There is nothing here to offend God or man.
GREATRAKES I am no Minister either, sir — and there is surely nothing to offend.
EVERARD Then come back tomorrow night and pay your penny like the rest of them.
GREATRAKES I regret that won't be possible — but I am happy to pay for what I have seen.

He proffers a pound coin. EVERARD *is astonished.*

EVERARD That is too much, sir.
GREATRAKES It is hardly enough — I have been greatly moved. Though if I may venture to be so bold, I should think one of the frothy comedies more suited to your intended audience. This parish has had a surfeit of tragedy.
EVERARD We are here to bear witness, sir — not to deceive. (*Begins to leave. The others follow*) Keep your money.
EUSTACIA My dear, that is no way to treat a gentleman. You must forgive my husband's churlishness, sir. He is often somewhat 'spleenish' on the eve of a performance. Allow us to introduce ourselves. Madam Eustacia and Mr Mathias Everard — and this, our Celebrated Theatre of Delights!
GREATRAKES Mr Valentine Greatrakes, Madam. (*Kisses her hand*) It is my very great pleasure.
EVERARD Mr Greatrakes. Your name goes before you. I had no idea we kept such distinguished company.
GREATRAKES Hardly distinguished.
EUSTACIA Greatrakes? You're that healer fellow, aren't you?
GREATRAKES I have been called worse, Madam.
EUSTACIA Why, then, of course distinguished! We came from London a month past, Mr Greatrakes — our annual excursion to the provinces. Your perform-

	ances at Lincoln's Inn were the talk of the town, were they not, Mathias?
EVERARD	You certainly caused a stir. Though I would hardly describe what Mr Greatrakes does as a performance.
EUSTACIA	Oh but it is, it must be! And leaves the modest efforts of us theatre folk quite in the shade. We have much in common, Mr Greatrakes. You must join us for supper and tell us all about this trick of yours.
GREATRAKES	It is not a trick, Madam Everard.
EUSTACIA	I see. (*Pause*) Then what is it?
GREATRAKES	I do not know. I thought I did but I am no longer sure.
EVERARD	And *I* am sure Mr Greatrakes has more to do with his time.
GREATRAKES	On the contrary, sir. I do not often enjoy such exotic company.
EVERARD	Yes. I daresay the exotic must have been at a premium in Mr Cromwell's army.
GREATRAKES	You know me too well, sir.
EVERARD	I know you not at all. You were the talk of the town, remember.
GREATRAKES	I was twelve when the theatres closed, Mr Everard.
EVERARD	You were not twelve when you fought under Cromwell's flag. The theatres were yet closed, Mr Greatrakes.
GREATRAKES	You will forgive me, sir, but I was not responsible for Mr Cromwell's every action.
EVERARD	Of course not. I imagine you never once thought about it. I had nineteen years to think about nothing else. My wife and I sold fish at Cheapside Market for nineteen years and I will never forgive Mr Cromwell or his foot-soldiers for that. But do you know, Mr Greatrakes, during all that time I was consoled by unassailable truths: they banned us because they were afraid; they silenced us because we were a voice for

those who had none; they broke our hearts because we *gave* heart to those whose hearts were broken; they crippled us because we could heal. (*Pause*) But we endured, Mr Greatrakes. We endured because we recognised that one day we would be necessary again.

GREATRAKES I am glad that day has come, Mr Everard. (*Places coin on ground*) I trust your play will bring some comfort here.

EVERARD (*A pause. Then as* GREATRAKES *leaves*) A moment, sir! (GREATRAKES *turns*) Our play had not quite finished. (*To* EUSTACIA) We will run the scene again from 'When youth is ripe'. (EUSTACIA *and the other actors stand by*) The epilogue, Mr Greatrakes, implies a form of resolution on stage which is not so readily found in life. And so, with respect to Mr Ford, I have dispensed with his and replaced it with the song Calantha commands as fitting for her end.

> EVERARD *gets into position as Nearchus and gestures to* EUSTACIA *to begin. They reprise the final scene, beginning with Armostes' 'When youth is ripe' and concluding with Nearchus' (*EVERARD*) 'The councils of the gods are never known, till men can call the effects of them their own.'*
>
> ANGEL LANDY *appears upstage. She comes to the altar. She looks at* GREATRAKES *who returns her stare. We hold this. Then she begins to sing. The song is 'in the play' but appears here to be addressed to* GREATRAKES, *who stands transfixed by the voice and by the girl whose instrument it is. The song ends as light fades on the girl who continues to watch* GREATRAKES *until, it seems, she disappears. The actors leave the stage.* EVERARD *and* GREATRAKES *alone.*

EVERARD You are troubled, sir.

GREATRAKES (*In tears*) Yes. Yes, but I know not why. It is but a play, the child's but a pretty voice. I know not why it moves me so.
EVERARD Then be content to know it does. There *are* mysteries, Mr Greatrakes. You must know that more than most.
GREATRAKES Who is she?
EVERARD Why do you need to know?
GREATRAKES I could never have seen her before but she is entirely familiar. It is as though my heart remembers her.
EVERARD Then let your heart tell you who she is — for I do not know.
GREATRAKES Please, Mr Everard — do not trifle with me. I ask but her name.
EVERARD As if that would be enough. (*Silence*) Her name is Angel Landy. I know that much because I christened her thus.
GREATRAKES Then she is your child by another name?
EVERARD She is nobody's child. She is a foundling, Mr Greatrakes. When your Lord Cromwell closed our doors, he did not entirely silence us. Once a year, on Midsummer's Eve, a company of actors would repair under cover of darkness to the village of Landy in the County of Surrey. There is a forest at the edge of that village and in the dead of night we would enter that forest and journey towards its heart. The following evening we would give a single performance of Mr Shakespeare's *A Midsummer Night's Dream*. There would be no audience; we would perform only for ourselves. It was at once a mute protest, a reminder and a form of preparation for a time we knew would come when we would be called on again. Twelve years ago, on such a night, the play had just ended when some of our number heard a child's voice singing some distance into the wood. We listened in wonder as the voice grew closer and closer until finally the child appeared

at the edge of the clearing we had just performed in. She was naked, bruised and bleeding, but she continued to sing as, one by one, she took us in, before settling her gaze on the light from the single lantern which accompanied our journey. That child was Angel Landy, sir, and the song you have just heard was the song she sang that night.

GREATRAKES Praise God for her deliverance, Mr Everard. The girl had good fortune to find you.

EVERARD Or was it our good fortune to find her?

GREATRAKES But what did she tell you about her circumstance?

EVERARD She told us nought. She could not speak. She had no memory. She could only sing, Mr Greatrakes. I daresay that was enough, wouldn't you?

GREATRAKES I must hear her again.

EVERARD Then you must return tomorrow night.

GREATRAKES I cannot be with the crowds.

EVERARD Why not, Mr Greatrakes?

GREATRAKES Because they clamour for my touch. And I do not have it to give.

EVERARD Then you will not hear the child sing again, will you?

GREATRAKES You must bring her to my house.

EVERARD No.

GREATRAKES I will pay you well for it.

EVERARD I said no, sir. She cannot be purchased, no more than she can be given away. Her place is here, Mr Greatrakes. (*Pause*) It is for you to resolve where yours lies.

EVERARD *leaves.* GREATRAKES *is alone.* ANGEL's *voice again. He turns to it.* ANGEL *appears half lit in the forest. She watches him as she sings. He goes towards her. She is gone.* MADAM EUSTACIA *appears.* GREATRAKES *looks at her. She returns his stare as the song continues 'front of house'.* GREATRAKES *exits.* EUSTACIA *crosses to where the coin lies. Picks it up. Pockets the coin and exits as lights fade.*

Scene Four

Greatrakes' castle. Evening. Four days later. A SERVANT *girl working at an open fire.* MICHAEL, *dressed in Greatrakes' cloak and with a freshly-starched shirt, enters, reciting Ithocles' speech from Act Two, Scene Two of* The Broken Heart.

MICHAEL Ambition! 'tis of vipers breed; it gnaws
A passage through the womb that gave it motion.
(*Jumps onto chair*)
Ambition like a seeled dove, mounts upward,
Higher and higher still, to perch on clouds
But tumbles headlong down with heavier ruin.
So squibs and crackers fly into the air
Then, only breaking with a noise, they vanish
In stench and smoke. Morality applied to
Timely practice, keeps the soul in tune,
At whose sweet music all our actions dance!

LIZZIE *enters.*

LIZZIE (*Unbuttoning her coat. To* MICHAEL) There'll be sweet music if the Master catches you wearin' his cloak. (*To* SERVANT) You. Go to the children's chamber. Fetch the swaddling from Mary's bed. Bring it to the Mistress in the barn.
SERVANT Why, Lizzie?
LIZZIE Because I say so.

SERVANT *exits.*

(*To* MICHAEL) Take that cloak off now before the Master gets back.
MICHAEL He'll be a while yet, the way the cripples is pullin' an' draggin' out of him beyond at the playactors' tent. (*Taking cloak off*) Isn't he the darin' man though, Lizzie? To be bravin' the play every night, sittin' shoulder to shoulder with the

     lot of them and him with eyes only for the doin's above on the stage.
LIZZIE He's the darin' man, all right.
MICHAEL Sparta now is where it all happens. Over the far side of the world is where you'll find that place, Lizzie. But do you know what? As faraway as it is, the connivin's and the skullduggery is the very same in that quarter as you'll find in these parts. You wouldn't think that now, would ye?
LIZZIE You would not.
MICHAEL The names, now, is different, of course. Amyclas and Ithocles and Calantha and the like. Ithocles, now, is my man. He does die fierce bravely every night, Lizzie. Strapped to a chair and stabbed to death by that oul' bastard Orgilus. This is my fourth night following on, Lizzie. You'll have to go yourself. Tomorrow night's the last and you'd be sorry to miss it.
LIZZIE I have more on my mind than playactin'.
MICHAEL I wish you would, though. For it *is* a wonder, Lizzie. I did think this parish was very small altogether but now I'm not so sure. For I'm inclined to think every man's story is a gallant one when it's told upon a stage.

     GREATRAKES *enters.* LIZZIE *looks at him.*

     I'm for the bed now, Master. For I do find that play fierce drainin' on the skull.
GREATRAKES (*As* MICHAEL *goes*) And on the heart, Michael?

     MICHAEL *stops.*

     What of the heart?
MICHAEL (*Perplexed*) Oh, that too, Master. Shur 'twould burn a hole in it.

     MICHAEL *exits.*

GREATRAKES He is greatly taken.
LIZZIE 'Tis a passing fancy only.
GREATRAKES Do you think so?
LIZZIE We'll see.
GREATRAKES Yes. But not for you, I gather.
LIZZIE No, Master. I'm not inclined to it.
GREATRAKES Nor Mistress Greatrakes, either.
LIZZIE No, Master. The Mistress and me are just back from the funeral.
GREATRAKES What funeral?
LIZZIE The man who died in the stables was buried today in Lismore.
GREATRAKES I see. And where is the Mistress, presently?
LIZZIE She is in the barn, Master.
GREATRAKES What does she do there?
LIZZIE She goes among the crowd. Them that are most sickly she tends to. Them that are troubled she prays with.
GREATRAKES Prays? With the Papists?
LIZZIE With whoever wishes. The Mistress says it's the one God in times of trouble.
GREATRAKES Does she? And do you pray with them?
LIZZIE Sometimes. I must go there now.
GREATRAKES What do you pray for?
LIZZIE That God will make them whole again. That God will heal them.
GREATRAKES That *I* will, you mean.
LIZZIE The Mistress bids the crowd pray for you also, Master. They know you are not well.
GREATRAKES I have nothing to give them, Lizzie. I know it in my heart.
LIZZIE It will come back, Master.
GREATRAKES Will it?

THOMAS *enters.*

THOMAS Madam Everard is in the hall, sir.
GREATRAKES Show her in, Thomas.
THOMAS Yes, sir.

THOMAS *exits.*

GREATRAKES I play while my wife prays. Things have come to a pretty pass, Lizzie.
LIZZIE I'm sure there's good reason, Master.

LIZZIE *exits as* THOMAS *returns with* EUSTACIA.

GREATRAKES Madam Everard. Thank you for coming to see me.
EUSTACIA It is my pleasure, sir. And how could one refuse the entreaties of this lovely man?
THOMAS I do my best, Ma'am.
EUSTACIA You certainly do.
THOMAS Can I get you some cider, Ma'am?
EUSTACIA Cider?
GREATRAKES We have no call for strong drink in this house.
EUSTACIA I see. (*Without conviction*) Would that more could say it, sir. Cider it will be, then.

THOMAS *exits.*

GREATRAKES Your Calantha was magnificent this evening, Madam Everard.
EUSTACIA My Calantha was competent, Mr Greatrakes. What do you think *they* made of it, though? The wretches, I mean.
GREATRAKES They were hanging on your every word, Madam.
EUSTACIA I have never seen a play fix a lame leg.
GREATRAKES No. Though it may heal a fractured spirit.
EUSTACIA Do you think so? You're worse than my husband. He believes that too, you know.
GREATRAKES And you don't?
EUSTACIA I believe in very little, Mr Greatrakes. You know, all those years the theatres were dark, my husband never once doubted that our time would come again. He had an unshakeable conviction that our work had some kind of sacred purpose and was therefore ultimately indispensable. There

was no particular day but at some point during our forced exile in Cheapside, I realised I didn't share that conviction. What was worse, I discovered I never had. I had a talent, yes, to strut and posture — but little else. I am a trickster, you see. Not like Mathias. He has a gift. His faith *is* his gift. You should remember that, Mr Greatrakes. (*Pause*) And I? Well, I have faith in him, don't I? That's something, I suppose.

GREATRAKES You are an honest woman, Madam Everard.

EUSTACIA Yes, I imagine I am — it saves so much time and bother.

THOMAS *returns with cider.*

Thank you, Thomas.

THOMAS *exits.*

I believe you are honest, also, Mr Greatrakes — so now you must tell me, why am I here?

GREATRAKES I am not sure, Madam.

EUSTACIA You are not sure of very much, are you?

GREATRAKES No, not anymore. I had a faith once, such as your husband's. (*Laughs ironically*) That God, in His infinite wisdom, had chosen me as an instrument of His mercy to His suffering children! I knew not why and cared not to question why. I did not seek it but I *had* been chosen and I would do His will. Six months ago, when I sailed for your country, my faith in that gift was as unshakeable as your husband's in his, but today it trembles like a leaf. There are two thousand souls beyond my door. They are screaming, not for God's mercy but for mine, and I do not have it to give. Because I have joined their ranks, Madam. They do not know it but I am one of them now.

EUSTACIA You have my sympathy, Mr Greatrakes.

GREATRAKES I need more than that from you.

EUSTACIA I do not know what I have to give.
GREATRAKES You have the child, Madam. (*Pause*) Angel Landy.
EUSTACIA What about her?

Silence.

GREATRAKES I don't know, Madam, but I must find out.
EUSTACIA Mr Greatrakes. I intend no disrespect but you are talking entirely in riddles.
GREATRAKES Forgive me. I have been, this week, five times to your tent, Madam.
EUSTACIA I am aware of it, sir. And I know it has cost you a pretty sum, for my husband tells me you paid for every seat your cripples occupied, in addition to your own. We are very grateful.
GREATRAKES It will take more than a few pounds to acquit a guilty conscience but that is another matter. I intend no disrespect to you either when I say that it was neither you nor Mr Ford's play compelled me to that tent.
EUSTACIA I left my vanity in Cheapside many years ago — I daresay Mr Ford's can take care of itself, too. But do you mean to say it was the child drew you back?
GREATRAKES Yes, Madam. I know it.

Silence.

EUSTACIA What do you want from her?
GREATRAKES When first I heard her, my heart remembered her from some very distant place. No, not her. Her voice. I believe it may be God's music she sings — the sweet chords of first innocence, the first sound that was ever made upon the earth. (*Pause*) I desire to make the child's acquaintance, Madam.
EUSTACIA I'm afraid that won't be possible.
GREATRAKES Why not?

44

EUSTACIA   My husband would not allow it.
GREATRAKES   I have no design upon the girl.
EUSTACIA   I believe you, Mr Greatrakes.
GREATRAKES   Then you must entreat with your husband on my behalf.
EUSTACIA   Angel Landy is not your saviour. Whatever troubles you will not be assuaged by a song. What you heard was a ditty sang upon the wind — worth nothing and instantly forgotten.

> RUTH *and* LIZZIE *enter, carrying a basin and some bloodied sheets.*

RUTH   I did not know you had company.
GREATRAKES   Madam Everard, my wife Ruth. Ruth, this is Madam Eustacia Everard from the Celebrated Theatre of Delights.
EUSTACIA   How do you do, Madam?
RUTH   I am well — all things considered. (*A glance to* GREATRAKES) Though a poor hostess to be sure — I did not expect you, Madam.
EUSTACIA   Your husband invited me.
RUTH   (*To* GREATRAKES) You should have told me. We might have offered more than cider.
EUSTACIA   I have been well provided for, I assure you, Madam. And have learned a great deal from your husband.
RUTH   (*As she takes off bloodied apron and gloves.* LIZZIE *takes these and leaves*) He is a veritable fountain of knowledge. I am sorry to have missed your play, Madam Everard. I'm afraid I was otherwise occupied.
EUSTACIA   You missed very little. *The Broken Heart* is not for the faint of heart.
RUTH   Then my husband must have a very strong heart. For he has been to-ing and fro-ing to your tent all week and seems to think of little else but the drama.
EUSTACIA   Indeed. Now, if you will excuse me —

RUTH (*As* LIZZIE *returns with basin of water and flannel.* RUTH *washes her hands*) No, please don't go. I thirst for civilised company, Madam — we see so little of it here in Affane. Isn't it true, Valentine?
GREATRAKES Yes, Ruth. It is true.
RUTH It certainly is! My father's a knight, you know. Holds a thousand acres down in Cornwall. And my brother is the King's Ambassador to the Court of Madrid. So I did, at one time, enjoy the benefits of civilised company. Until I met Valentine, that is, and we ended up here. (LIZZIE *exits*) Here in squalid little, disease infested, Affane.
EUSTACIA I am sorry you feel you have stooped so low, Madam Greatrakes. I do have to go now.
RUTH Yes, back to the drama! We have our own here too, you know. In the minor key, I grant you, but compelling nonetheless. Some days ago, a death, today an anonymous funeral and (*To* GREATRAKES) just now, with what savage irony, my darling, a child born in a stable. (*To* EUSTACIA) Nothing to compare with the drama on your stage, Madam Everard, but, yes, compelling in its own sordid little way.
EUSTACIA I do not doubt it. Our theatre seldom compares with the drama of the real world. Does it, Mr Greatrakes? (*Pause*) You were asking about angels. Personally, I do not credit their existence but one that goes by that name is sometimes found walking in the forest at dead of night. If you believe in angels, you should seek yours there. (*To* RUTH) Until we meet again, Madam.
RUTH I do not think we will meet again.

EUSTACIA *leaves. Silence.*

(*To* GREATRAKES) What? I should fall to my knees and beg your forgiveness? You'll wait for it.
GREATRAKES I do not wait for it.

RUTH   No. Because you do not care.
GREATRAKES   It is true. I do not care! Leave me now!
RUTH   Not before I see you cross that yard and tell *them* you do not care. Spare them, at least, the illusion of hope. (*Pause*) Have you no shame, Valentine?
GREATRAKES   No! I have no shame! Now give my head peace and quit my sight!
RUTH   I will leave when I have said what I wish to say. (*Pause*) A child was born in your stables tonight whilst you frolicked at the play tent and pondered the existence of angels. The woman who gave birth travelled thirty miles to be here. She led her blind husband every step of the way. In the years to come she will tell that child the story of how they had journeyed in hope. But of how that hope was denied because the healer had grown weary of his gift and no longer cared! (*Pause*) Cross that yard and go to them, Valentine. If there is charity left in your heart, I dare you to cross that yard now and tell them that they must no longer hope!
GREATRAKES   I cannot!
RUTH   Why not? Too weary, even for that much? I thought I knew you, Valentine. Even in this dark hour I thought I knew you. But I will never know how you could sit in that tent and ignore all that you witnessed on your way there.
GREATRAKES   I do it because I must!
RUTH   Then cross that yard because you must! If you betray those people you will never find peace again.
GREATRAKES   I will heal when I am healed. I can do no more. You are so well versed on the subject of my charity, Ruth. Where is yours for me when it is so desperately needed?
RUTH   Where it always was. I know what this has cost you. Because I was there, Valentine. I was there for all of it. And you have paid no price that I did not pay also. I did bid you be silent. I begged you to walk away from what you found because I

47

knew what it would exact from us. But you embraced it. You embraced it because your heart would not countenance otherwise. And when you did, I did too. It was our *destiny*! We have sacrificed ourselves to it and if it destroys you it will surely consume me also. Perhaps we are doomed either way, but better it should destroy us in the honouring than be destroyed in the breach.
GREATRAKES I am trying, Ruth. God knows I am trying. I need more time.
RUTH What, for the playhouse? For your angels?
GREATRAKES Please. You must trust me.
RUTH I have always trusted you.
GREATRAKES Then do not fail me now. And if it be God's will I should heal again, then He will not fail us either. But if it *is* our destiny, Ruth, if it is *all* destiny, then God must account for what happened to me in London. For if it were not the gutter pamphleteers, it were the physics and the philosophers; if it were not the Ministers of our Church, it were his Majesty's henchmen. And if it were not all of those conjoined, it were — God forgive me — the poor afflicted themselves in their infinite relentless number. But between them all, they have stolen something, without which I can never hope to heal.
RUTH And what is that?
GREATRAKES My innocence, Ruth. Doing without knowing why. Doing without caring why. These hands an instrument only — mute servants to the miraculous. (*Pause*) You remember, don't you?
RUTH (*Pause*) Yes. I remember.
GREATRAKES Then wait for me.
RUTH The afflicted have waited too long, Valentine.
GREATRAKES Then perhaps that is *their* destiny. For I must have mine. I did not ordain it thus. But I must have it now.

Exits. End of Scene Four.

Scene Five

A wood near Affane. The following night. GREATRAKES *enters, far upstage. After a moment or two,* ANGEL *enters, wandering aimlessly into the space.* GREATRAKES *watches her.* ANGEL *becomes aware of his presence, though she does not look in his direction.*

GREATRAKES Angel.
ANGEL Yes, sir.
GREATRAKES (*Approaches tentatively*) Do not be afraid. I will not harm you.
ANGEL I am not afraid.
GREATRAKES Do you know who I am?
ANGEL (*Looks at him for the first time*) Yes. Have you come to heal me?
GREATRAKES I did not know you were sickly.
ANGEL The Mistress said you were looking for me.
GREATRAKES Yes. But I have not come to heal you.
ANGEL As you wish, sir.
GREATRAKES May I sit with you?
ANGEL I cannot stay long. The players are at the tavern. We must take the tent down when they return.
GREATRAKES That is heavy work for a young girl.
ANGEL I am very strong. And not so young. The Mistress and me pack the costumes. Then we put the benches in the wagons. Last it's feed and water the horses.
GREATRAKES When do you leave?
ANGEL At first light. The Master says we have a long journey.
GREATRAKES Where are you for?
ANGEL I do not know. I never know. It never matters.
GREATRAKES But you like your work?
ANGEL (*Quizzical*) It is what I do, sir.
GREATRAKES Yes. But do you enjoy to do it?
ANGEL I like to sing. (*Pause*) Sometimes, anyway.
GREATRAKES Only sometimes?
ANGEL Yes. (*Pause*) Do your children sing, sir?

GREATRAKES (*Surprised*) What?
ANGEL Do your children like to sing?
GREATRAKES Why, yes. When they are happy.
ANGEL Only when they are happy?
GREATRAKES They sing in church also.
ANGEL Are they not happy in church?
GREATRAKES (*Smiling*) Yes. I imagine they are.
ANGEL I do not go to church.
GREATRAKES No?
ANGEL Master Everard says the Theatre is our Church. He says we honour God in our work and let the Ministers honour Him in their chapel!
GREATRAKES And what do *you* say?
ANGEL I don't say anything. You must miss them sorely, Mr Greatrakes.
GREATRAKES Who?
LIZZIE Your children.
GREATRAKES Who told you about my children?
LIZZIE I heard some women talking in the village. They said the cripples frightened your children and so they had to leave. (*Pause*) Do they frighten you, Mr Greatrakes?
GREATRAKES Yes.
ANGEL Then you should tend to them. For if you did, they would go away and your children would come home and you would all live happily ever after.
GREATRAKES I wish it were that simple, Angel.
ANGEL Is it not, sir?
GREATRAKES No. It is something akin to singing. It is a gift.
ANGEL Is singing a gift?
GREATRAKES Yes. I believe it is.
ANGEL Who from, sir?
GREATRAKES From God, I believe.
ANGEL (*Pleased*) Oh. My song too?
GREATRAKES Yours especially. And when you have a gift, well sometimes you can use it well and other times not so well. And then sometimes you cannot use it at all.

ANGEL I must be singing all the time.
GREATRAKES Even if it does not please you?
ANGEL Especially when it does not please me!
GREATRAKES Why so?
ANGEL Because that is what I do, sir. I sing.
GREATRAKES Where did the song come from, Angel?
ANGEL Did you not just tell me, Mr Greatrakes? You said it were a gift from God.
GREATRAKES Your voice, yes. But the song itself. Where did you learn it?
ANGEL I do not know. Think you if my voice was God's gift, then the song might be also?
GREATRAKES It is possible. For sure it has no feel of this world about it. (*Pause*) Your song enchants me, Angel.
ANGEL Is that why you sent for me?
GREATRAKES It is why I asked for you. (*Pause*) Mr Everard told me how the song was on your lips when he found you.
ANGEL (*Smiling*) He calls it the song of the forest. Perhaps that is where it came from.
GREATRAKES Where did *you* come from, Angel?
ANGEL From the forest also, sir. You know as much.
GREATRAKES Yes. But how did you come to be there?
ANGEL I do not know. When Mistress Everard has had too much wine and is out of sorts, she says I must have been abandoned by tinsmiths. Perhaps it is so.
GREATRAKES I cannot think any would abandon you, Angel.
ANGEL Perhaps some poor mother in distress. One who had me in the forest out of wedlock and left me there in her shame.
GREATRAKES That could not be. Everard said you were some three or four years old when he found you. You could not have survived that long.
ANGEL Could I not, sir?
GREATRAKES It is not possible. You would have starved to death.
ANGEL (*Picks foliage from undergrowth*) Would you eat these, sir?
GREATRAKES No. Of course not.

ANGEL   I would. (*Pause*) Master Everard said I could not speak a word when he found me — only sing. (*Pause*) I do not know, sir. I did wonder but not anymore. Perhaps it was a day, perhaps a year. Perhaps I was always there.
GREATRAKES   We don't have much time, Angel. You must tell me everything you remember about the forest.
ANGEL   That won't take long, Mr Greatrakes — for I remember nothing.
GREATRAKES   Nothing?
ANGEL   Nothing at all, sir. Why do you wish to know?

Silence. EVERARD *enters.*

GREATRAKES   Angel, I believe God may have sent you to me. When you sing, I believe it may be that God speaks to me with your voice.
ANGEL   I cannot imagine, sir. I am just a foundling. But if it be true, is that not enough for you?
EVERARD   No. That would never be enough for Mr Greatrakes. He must have proof. He must poke his grubby little fingers in the wound. Well not here, sir. For if you have no faith, there is no proof either.
GREATRAKES   I am desperate, sir.
EVERARD   No. Look you to the crowds that line the road to your house if you seek to know desperation. Look you to them if you require to know faith. This child *is* what she *is*, sir. Take from it what you will. But you will dissect her no more!
GREATRAKES   I must hear her sing again. That is all I ask.
EVERARD   You have heard enough.
ANGEL   I do not mind to sing, Master.
EVERARD   I said no!
GREATRAKES   I implore you, Mr Everard, one last time.
EVERARD   Why, sir? To be sure? You cannot be sure! If you imagine God speaks to you through her, then He has already spoken and if she sing it a hundred times more it will not add to what you have

	already heard.
ANGEL	Let me sing for him, Master Everard. One last time.
EVERARD	No. Let him remember it, if he will. The child has her function, Mr Greatrakes. And if I may say so, you have yours. Come, Angel.
ANGEL	I am sorry, Mr Greatrakes.
GREATRAKES	It matters not. Goodbye, Angel.

> EVERARD *and* ANGEL *leave.* GREATRAKES *watches them go. Silence. He falls to his knees. Prays in silence. The prayer becomes a quiet wail of agony as his body arches over, his fists beating the forest floor.* RUTH *enters, unseen by* GREATRAKES. *She comes forward but is interrupted by the arrival of a young* MAN *and* WOMAN. *The* MAN *is blind, the* WOMAN *carries an infant in a blanket.*

WOMAN	(*Quietly*) Please, sir?

> GREATRAKES *doesn't hear. She goes forward a step.*

	Mr Greatrakes?
GREATRAKES	Who is it?
WOMAN	(*Coming forward again*) I am sorry to trouble you, sir.
GREATRAKES	What do you want?
WOMAN	My name is Ellen Reilly, sir. And beyond is my husband, Martin. And this is our baby was born in your stable last night.
GREATRAKES	Yes. I heard. Are you well?
WOMAN	I am, sir.
GREATRAKES	And the infant?
WOMAN	She thrives, sir. We're for calling her Ruth in honour of your wife. She showed us great kindness, sir.
GREATRAKES	My wife is a good woman.
WOMAN	She is, sir. And I know you are a good man. Beggin' your pardon, sir, but we did follow you from the house beyond, to the forest here. And

though I know you're not well and not fit for curin', I'm beggin' you, sir, to put hands on my poor Martin, that he might lay eyes on his beautiful baby.

GREATRAKES No. I cannot.
WOMAN (*Crying*) You must, Mr Greatrakes, you must!
GREATRAKES No! I tell you I am not able.
WOMAN If you'd only try, sir. Try is all we ask.
GREATRAKES I have no power to!
WOMAN Behold the child, sir.
GREATRAKES No! Leave me!
WOMAN Behold her lovely face, sir.
GREATRAKES I cannot!
WOMAN You must, sir! It is my husband cannot.

Quieter now. Pushes the infant under GREATRAKES' *face.*

Isn't she beautiful, sir?
GREATRAKES (*Silence. Looking at the child*) Yes. Praise God, she is. He blessed us with three of our own, you know. William and Edmund and Little Mary. They had to go away. Yes. But I pray God they will return safely. (*Looks at* MAN) Bring your husband to me.
WOMAN Thank you, sir. Thank you.

The WOMAN *goes to her husband.* GREATRAKES *sees* RUTH *for the first time. The* WOMAN *leads her husband downstage to* GREATRAKES.

GREATRAKES Do not be afraid. (*Lowers* MAN *to his knees. Touches his eyes*) May God Almighty heal thee for His mercy's sake.

Silence.

MAN I cannot see, sir.
GREATRAKES (*With increased intensity*) May God Almighty heal thee for His mercy's sake.

Silence.

MAN There is no change, sir. I see nothing.
GREATRAKES (*Desperate now*) May God Almighty heal thee for His mercy's sake. May God Almighty heal thee for His mercy's sake!
MAN There is nothing, sir. It is all dark!

Silence.

GREATRAKES Yes. All dark. I am sorry. I have failed you. Go home now.
WOMAN Please, sir —
GREATRAKES No! It is over! Leave me!
RUTH (*As* MAN *and* WOMAN *leave*) He will try again tomorrow.
WOMAN Thank you, sir. Thank you for trying.

They disappear into the forest.

RUTH The girl was right. You did try. That is all that matters.
GREATRAKES The boy will never set eyes on his child. *That* is all that matters.
RUTH They will return tomorrow. Not all are cured — that is as it has always been.
GREATRAKES These hands are not as they have always been. This heart is not as it was. Whatever I had I have lost, Ruth.
RUTH It will come back!
GREATRAKES When!
RUTH I do not know, but if you should fail a hundred times you must prevail now.
GREATRAKES I cannot!
RUTH In twenty minutes every soul in that yard will know what happened here.
GREATRAKES They will know I have failed.
RUTH They will know you tried.
GREATRAKES I have failed, Ruth!

RUTH You cannot give hope and take it away again.
GREATRAKES Then we must do as you say. We must set them free of hope. For I have lost mine.
RUTH When I saw you behold that infant's face just now, I remembered how it was for us before God called you to be His servant. I have often wished for those days, Valentine, and I know you have too.
GREATRAKES We can have them again, Ruth. In a few months no one will even remember my name.
RUTH No.
GREATRAKES Please, Ruth.
RUTH No! I cannot abide to live with the ghosts of those we will have betrayed. Their spirits will haunt us — and they will never let us rest.

Silence.

I received a letter today from my father. The children pine for us.
GREATRAKES Then we must bring them home.
RUTH I will go to them.
GREATRAKES Bring them back, Ruth.
RUTH I will bring them back when you come back. I do not know where you are going but I can no longer journey with you.

RUTH *leaves.* GREATRAKES *alone. After a moment or two we hear* ANGEL's *voice in the distance.* GREATRAKES *becomes aware of it. Turns to look for her but there is no one there.*

GREATRAKES Angel? (*Pause*) Angel! (*Pause*) Angel!

Cut to black as the music continues. End of Act One.

ACT TWO

Scene One

Greatrakes' castle. Some days later. We open with THOMAS *alone on stage. He is seated at the table, meticulously entering figures into a large ledger-type book. A servant enters laden with a basket of soiled sheets, bandages etc. The* SERVANT *lays these down before leaving again and this procession from the yard to the house may continue under the Scene which follows.* MICHAEL *enters, also carrying a basket which he sets down.*

THOMAS   Well?
MICHAEL   'Tis done. I just seen the last of them to the gate. Affane is near emptied too. They've been pouring out of the hostel since first light. To see them walkin' back them roads like that and the same disorder on them as brought them here in the first place — 'twould break your heart, so it would.
THOMAS   I find mine remains intact, Michael.
MICHAEL   You must have a heart of stone so — the same as the Master above in his chamber.
THOMAS   You may judge the constitution of my heart, Michael — but not the Master's.
MICHAEL   No. A better man than me will do that. (*Pause*) 'Tis fierce quiet in the yard after them.
THOMAS   I am pleased to hear it.
MICHAEL   Have you no pity at all for the poor wretches?
THOMAS   And what use, pray tell, would they put it to if I had? Pity is a base currency, Michael. I neither offer or seek it.
MICHAEL   Aisy say as much and you sittin' in here, Thomas. If you'd stood in that yard all day and watched them leave, you would not be as free.

57

THOMAS Perhaps not. But I did not stand in the yard, Michael. And it was not your place to do so either. We are not charged with having opinions. Our function here is to maintain good order. And now our 'guests' have departed we must labour to restore that order. You may start with the malthouse at first light.

LIZZIE enters.

Lizzie. Back safely, I trust.

LIZZIE (*Takes off coat*) Aye. I was delayed by the crowds comin' again' me on the road home. The horse and carriage is at Osborne's yet, Michael.

MICHAEL I'll go for them presently — there's room and plenty here for them now.

THOMAS Your brother pines for our departed guests, Lizzie.

LIZZIE I will miss them also.

MICHAEL I do not pine. I was only saying —

THOMAS What you were saying is of no consequence now, Michael.

MICHAEL Not to you maybe. I respect you, Thomas, and I respect the Master also —

THOMAS We are entirely gratified.

MICHAEL But I won't be told what to think by either of you.

LIZZIE Michael!

THOMAS Then you may consider your position here.

MICHAEL I will if I must but I will not be muzzled. You saw them on the road beyond, Lizzie. I know what trouble they brought us but it was nothing to their own troubles. They say the Master tried to heal the blind man in the forest. They say he failed, but all any of them asked was that he try again. I think he was too proud.

THOMAS That's enough, boy!

MICHAEL He should have tried, Thomas — he owed them that much.

THOMAS What do you know what your Master owes to

MICHAEL any? Fit you better to consider what you owe him.
He cured me and I am grateful for it but he did not buy my silence. I remember what it was like to be deformed. You know it also, Thomas.
THOMAS That is no concern of yours — you will not quote me for your purpose.
MICHAEL No, I won't. Because I have heard you in the tavern in your cups. How one time, when the Master offered, you told him you did not wish to be cured.
THOMAS Aye. And I did not.
MICHAEL D'ye mark it, Lizzie? 'At home in this battered vessel,' says he. Well, good luck to you, Thomas. But you had a choice. Them cripples did not.
LIZZIE It matters not now, Michael, for it is too late. Go to Osborne's for the carriage.
MICHAEL I will go when I'm ready. I will go when the last cripple has left the road, for I cannot bear to set eyes on them again.
THOMAS Methinks all that playactin' has rubbed off on your brother, Lizzie. Put your heart back in its chamber, boy. For we have seen it now and we know it breaks. But know you this, no heart breaks more than your Master's. I fought with him in Cromwell's army. Saw him give quarter to the Papists when he might have burnt them to ashes in their garrison. Watched him feed the Royalist prisoners with his own rations when our Colonel would have them starve. And do you know why? Because he were a good man before he were a good soldier. And he did not forget that when many men did. Them that begged him for his touch — not one of them suffers more tonight than he does. And if he could have cured them, he surely would.
MICHAEL Then why did he not try again?
THOMAS How in God's name should I know? I am a simple man, Michael — a poor foot-soldier that never found his way home from your god-

59

forsaken country. But I know this — a man's heart has more secret corners than there are stars in the sky. I'll warrant the answer to your question lies in one of them corners. (*Closes ledger. Puts it away*) How fared the Mistress on the road to the boat, Lizzie?

LIZZIE As you would imagine she fared.

MICHAEL Is she not coming back, Lizzie?

LIZZIE She said not one word along the way. And only this at the dockside: that the Master was not well, that we must take care to mind him.

THOMAS We will do no less, Lizzie.

LIZZIE Did he leave his chamber today?

THOMAS No. Hardly at all these last few days.

LIZZIE He must eat, Thomas.

THOMAS He'll eat when he is hungry. And the Mistress will return when she sees fit, Michael — her and her children with her. In the meanwhile we must make this estate fit for their return. That is all we can do.

MICHAEL (*A moment. Then, resolved*) Very well so. I will go to Osborne's for the carriage. I will start on the malthouse the instant I get back.

THOMAS One step at a time, Michael. Go to Osborne's. I'll see you in the tavern when you get back. I might even buy you a tankard.

MICHAEL That'll be the first miracle around here in a long time. (*Takes folio from trouser pocket*) Did I show you this, Lizzie?

LIZZIE What is it?

MICHAEL Mr Everard gave it to me. It's the play they were doing in the tent last week.

LIZZIE That was very kind of him.

MICHAEL I do miss *them* too, Lizzie. Sometimes I do wonder was it only a dream — did they pass this way at all?

LIZZIE It was not a dream, Michael. Go on now, or you'll be comin' home in the dark.

MICHAEL Very well so. (*Takes script back*) I'll see yis later.

MICHAEL *exits.*

LIZZIE I met Mistress Osborne when I brought the carriage back to the yard.
THOMAS That must have made your day.
LIZZIE She offered me a position, Thomas.
THOMAS Did she indeed? And what did you say to that?
LIZZIE I told her I was perfectly happy where I was. (*Pause*) I lied to her, Thomas.
THOMAS Of course you did.
LIZZIE I wanted to go.
THOMAS But you did not. (*Pause*) Because you are an old soldier like myself. You may not have the insignia but you know what loyalty is, don't you?
LIZZIE Is that why you stayed?
THOMAS He is an honourable man, Lizzie. I've never come across that before, in or out of uniform, and I'll never know why but it appeals to me. (*Laughs*) I have no honour, Lizzie. I am not decent. I could not shed a tear for cripples if my life depended on it. But there is something wholesome about a proximity to goodness — even if I could never quite live with it myself.
LIZZIE I only wish we knew how to help him.
THOMAS No man may carry another's cross, Lizzie. Or woman, either. All you can do is walk beside him — and pick him up when he falls!

GREATRAKES *enters.*

Sir! It is good to see you up.
GREATRAKES Not before time, I'll warrant.
THOMAS It is never too late, sir — there is light yet in the sky.
GREATRAKES Yes. How was your journey, Lizzie?
LIZZIE (*A glance at* THOMAS) It was pleasant.
GREATRAKES And my wife?
LIZZIE She was peaceful.

GREATRAKES Good. Let us hope she travels safely.
THOMAS The sea was calm, sir — was it not, Lizzie?
LIZZIE (*Picking up the hint*) Why, yes, Master — she will have fair crossing.
GREATRAKES I hope so. (*Pause*) Why so quiet in the yard, Thomas?
THOMAS The crowds have gone, sir.
GREATRAKES All of them?
THOMAS Yes, sir. The village also. They have all gone.
GREATRAKES (*To* LIZZIE) Did my wife inspire this?
LIZZIE Yes, Master. She went among them last evening and bid them disperse.
GREATRAKES What did she tell them?
LIZZIE That you were sickly and could no longer practise.
GREATRAKES And that satisfied them?
LIZZIE It must have, Master.

Silence.

GREATRAKES Then it is over?
THOMAS (*A glance at* LIZZIE) Yes, sir. It is over.

GREATRAKES *opens his front door.*

GREATRAKES The air of liberation is not as sweet as I had anticipated. (*Without turning*) I wonder why that is, Lizzie.
LIZZIE I do not know, sir. Will you take supper now?
GREATRAKES No.
LIZZIE You have not eaten all week, Master.
GREATRAKES I have no appetite just now.
THOMAS The Master will eat when he is hungry, Lizzie.
LIZZIE No! If he does not eat he will die. Mistress Greatrakes did not lie to the crowds, sir. You are not well. She said we must take care of you but we cannot if you will not eat.
GREATRAKES I will eat tomorrow, Lizzie.
LIZZIE Very well so.

She begins to leave.

GREATRAKES Lizzie.
LIZZIE Yes, sir?

Silence.

GREATRAKES I am sorry.
LIZZIE For what, sir?
GREATRAKES For all that has unfolded here.
LIZZIE You owe us no apology, sir.
GREATRAKES Yes, I do. And a great deal more. You have all paid dearly for what I subscribed to. If I had known then what you would be forced to endure, I would have bid God look elsewhere. One way or the other, it is over now and we must look forward. We had lives before this — all of us — and we shall have them again, I promise. (*Pause*) My wife will soon return. You know this, don't you?
THOMAS It goes without saying, sir.
GREATRAKES It does not go without saying, Thomas. That is why I am saying it.
THOMAS Yes, sir.
GREATRAKES She *will* return. And our children with her.
LIZZIE We do not doubt it, sir.
GREATRAKES You *may* not doubt it. For I cannot. Before she returns, I intend that this estate be restored to good order.
THOMAS I was just saying as much to Michael, sir. We'll start with the malthouse at first light.
GREATRAKES The malthouse will be razed to the ground at first light.
THOMAS I beg your pardon, sir?
GREATRAKES You heard me. The barn and stables to follow.
THOMAS But why, sir?
GREATRAKES Because I ordain it! Burn everything! Not a shed left standing. I want no sign that those wretches ever set foot here, do you understand? (*Silence*)

Do you!
THOMAS Yes, sir. I understand.
LIZZIE And I do not. Forgive me, sir, but you cannot burn memory.
GREATRAKES No. But I can burn everything else. If it is over, it is over. And if we cannot burn memory we will not feed its flame. From this night on, there is to be no account of what took place here. No talk of God or cripples or cures. Nothing, do you hear?

MICHAEL enters, breathless and excited.

MICHAEL Mr Greatrakes! Mr Greatrakes! The playactors is back!
GREATRAKES What are you saying, boy?
MICHAEL You heard me, Master. The playactors! They're beyond at the back door — askin' to know if they can see yourself.
GREATRAKES Which players are they?
MICHAEL Mr Everard, Master. Mr Everard and the young wan with him. The one they call Angel, Master.

Silence.

GREATRAKES What do they want?
MICHAEL I do not know, Master.
GREATRAKES (*A glance at* LIZZIE) Show them in.

MICHAEL goes out and returns instantly with EVERARD and ANGEL, who is subdued and withdrawn.

Mr Everard, I had not expected to see you again.
EVERARD I will not lie to you, sir — I had no design to. Sit you down, Angel.
GREATRAKES To what do I owe the honour, Mr Everard?
EVERARD It is the child, sir. She is not well.
GREATRAKES She does look poorly. What ails you, Angel?
ANGEL (*Her voice is noticeably weakened*) I do not know, sir.

EVERARD　We have been playing this week past in the town of Waterford. Our play was as you found it here, our tent was full and our company in good spirits. Two nights ago, at the close, it came Angel's turn to sing. But when she stepped forward and drew breath, she found she could not. I motioned to her to begin again. And so she did but no sound came from her throat. She may speak, sir, but cannot sing and has been that way since.

GREATRAKES　Did you bring her to a physick?

EVERARD　We have met three, sir, and all have examined her. They say her vocal chords are perfectly intact and can offer no explanation why she may not sing.

GREATRAKES　Let me see. Bring a candle, Lizzie. Open your mouth, Angel. (*Holds candle over, looks inside her mouth, touching her throat with his fingers etc.*) Does this hurt? (*She shakes her head*) Or this? (*She shakes again*) Open further now — wide as you can. (*Pause*) Thank you, Angel. (*To* EVERARD) For sure there is no sign of any fever or inflammation. I am no physick, sir, but can find no explanation either.

EVERARD　I have not come thirty miles on horseback for explanation, Mr Greatrakes.

GREATRAKES　Then why have you come?

EVERARD　I warrant you know why. You must cure the child, sir.

GREATRAKES　No. No, I cannot.

EVERARD　You must. You know you must.

GREATRAKES　No! It is over! This house is mine again. Did you not see them on the road? They have gone, sir. They have gone because they know it is over.

EVERARD　I saw them right enough. And a pitiful sight they were too. But this child was not of their number. She stands before you and you cannot refuse her.

GREATRAKES　I cannot cure her! Think you I would refuse her out of malice?

EVERARD No, sir, I do not. I believe you are afraid. I believe you have honest doubt. But you must resolve it now. And if it be too late for the caravan along that road, it is not too late for us.

GREATRAKES No. I am sorry. I must ask you to leave. I cannot help the child.

EVERARD (*Takes purse from pocket*) There are ten guineas in this purse. It is yours if you will but try to heal her.

GREATRAKES (*Rages*) Keep your purse! Ten times that would change nothing! I never did this for money!

EVERARD Then do it for what money cannot buy! (*Pause*) In that forest last week, I heard you tell Angel you believed God may have sent her to you. When she sings, you said you believe God speaks to you in her voice. If that be so, then let her sing, Mister — and let your God speak to you again.

GREATRAKES It is too late for that. God spoke once to me before and I have had nought but affliction since. God, in His infinite mercy, purloined my wife and children. He has exhausted my servants and driven me to the very edge of despair. If I never hear of God again, I shall die a happy man. (*Turns from them*) Now, quit my sight and leave me be!

Silence. GREATRAKES *begins to leave.*

ANGEL Please, sir? (*Pause*) I wish to sing again. (*Pause*) It is all I can do.

Silence. They watch GREATRAKES. *Eventually he turns, looks at* ANGEL, *then looks at the others. He approaches* ANGEL.

GREATRAKES (*First brushes her hair fondly with his hand. Then lowers her to her knees and places both hands on her throat*) May God Almighty . . . (*He falters. Looks at* LIZZIE, *then to* EVERARD, *then back to* ANGEL) May

God Almighty heal thee for His mercy's sake. May God Almighty heal thee for His mercy's sake! (*Silence. He withdraws his hands*) Sing, Angel. Sing!

ANGEL looks appealingly at GREATRAKES. Afraid to try. He nods at her encouragingly. Looks up. Takes a breath. Tries to sing. Fails. Tries again, repeatedly. Only a series of strange cries emerge, joining to become one single howl of agony. She falls to the ground.

ANGEL I cannot! I cannot! I cannot!
GREATRAKES (*To EVERARD*) Are you satisfied, sir?
EVERARD Are you, Mr Greatrakes?
GREATRAKES I am sorry, Angel.

Silence.

LIZZIE The girl must stay with us. The Master will try again tomorrow.
EVERARD Our company sets sail for England at first light. Angel must travel with us.
LIZZIE No. She will return when she is well. The Master will try again tomorrow. And again the next until she is well.
EVERARD What say you, sir?
GREATRAKES (*Looking at LIZZIE*) I do not appear to have a choice in the matter.
LIZZIE (*Goes to ANGEL*) Come, Angel, you must be tired after your journey. I'll show you to your chamber.

LIZZIE begins to lead ANGEL off. ANGEL stops. Turns to EVERARD.

EVERARD (*Embraces ANGEL*) It will not be for long, Angel.

ANGEL looks from EVERARD to GREATRAKES, then exits with LIZZIE.

THOMAS (*To* EVERARD) It is near dark, sir. Will you stay the night?
EVERARD Thank you, but we sail on the morning tide.
THOMAS Very well, sir. I'll see your horse is fed and watered before you go. Come along, Michael.
MICHAEL Mr Everard?
EVERARD Yes, Michael?
MICHAEL You must not fret now. We'll take good care of Angel, sir.
EVERARD I am sure you will.

MICHAEL *nods and exits.*

(*To* GREATRAKES) I thank you, sir.
GREATRAKES I promise nothing, Mr Everard. You know that.
EVERARD I know. And something I want *you* to know, Mr Greatrakes. What I told you about Mr Cromwell barring the doors of the playhouses. How I never doubted our time would come again. I was lying. I did doubt. Not a day passed when I did not. And what I doubted was not that we would open again, or that we would one day be necessary again. I doubted if, when the time came, we would still be *able*, if our enforced silence hadn't somehow corroded us. There was no way of assuaging that doubt. We had no choice but to wait until that silence was lifted to see if we could speak again. (*Pause*) Goodbye, Mr Greatrakes.

EVERARD *leaves.* GREATRAKES *watches him go. Goes to front door. Opens double doors. A blast of light to meet him. The girl's voice on cue. Lights fade to end of scene.*

Scene Two

Greatrakes' castle. Two weeks later. Evening. As lights come up, LIZZIE *and the* SERVANT *girl cover the oak table with an ornate, richly textured tablecloth. Then* LIZZIE *begins to set the table for dinner.* THOMAS *enters with a flourish, carrying a basin and cloth in one hand and a pair of shining boots in the other.*

THOMAS (*As he enters*) Opus finitum est. Benedicat Deus operas!
LIZZIE Try that in the King's English.
THOMAS The work is finished. May God bless the workmen! (*Pours cider*) And thirsty work it is too, Lizzie.
LIZZIE He may bless the workmen but I doubt He'll bless the work. I have never seen the like of it for waste.
THOMAS We do only as we are bid, Elizabeth! One malthouse, one barn and one stable burnt to the ground and raised, like Lazarus from the dead, in two weeks! That is no mean achievement — whatever the logic.
LIZZIE Greatrakes' Folly, the workmen call it.
THOMAS If it be folly they have been well rewarded for it. (*Takes off shirt, pours water into basin and begins to wash*) And if it please the Master, then who are we to judge it wise or foolish!
LIZZIE Aye. If it please the Master. Did you find Michael?
THOMAS Perched atop a haystack in the river field, reciting that infernal play again. The boy is no actor, Lizzie.
LIZZIE He may dream, may he not?
THOMAS Oh, yes. And well versed he is in that regard. (*Puts on a freshly-starched shirt*) What do you think?
LIZZIE You'll do.
THOMAS Is that all? I fancied you'd fall to a weakness at the sight of me.
LIZZIE Well you fancied wrong. 'Twill take more than a starched shirt to impress me, Thomas Wyvern.

THOMAS What say you to my boots then?
LIZZIE I say they are the Master's.
THOMAS (*Somewhat crestfallen. Puts them on*) Yes. D'you think he'll notice?
LIZZIE The Master has eyes for precious little these days.
THOMAS True. Shouldn't you be getting ready?
LIZZIE I am as ready as I wish to be.
THOMAS I mean no disrespect, Lizzie, but it's not every day we are called to the Master's table.
LIZZIE I did not ask to eat with him. He can take me as I am or not at all.
THOMAS To what do we owe the honour, anyway?
LIZZIE He did not say. Just that he was going to Lismore for the day and we must dine with him on his return.
THOMAS Is the girl with him?
LIZZIE They cannot be separated.
THOMAS Why should they be? She is his guest, is she not?
LIZZIE She is his patient.
THOMAS Aye. And he must cure her. So he must spend time with her.
LIZZIE He has done everything *but* cure her.
THOMAS You have seen it with your own eyes, Lizzie. Not a day passes he does not try.
LIZZIE Yes. And not a day passes he does not walk with her in the forest, or sail with her on the river. She is not here to take the air, Thomas.
THOMAS No. But what harm if she do?
LIZZIE None — if she is alone. It is not wholesome. That is all I say.
THOMAS And well you say no more then, Lizzie.
LIZZIE Better speak now than when it is too late.
THOMAS Yes. And better not put flesh where there is no bone.
LIZZIE (*Takes letter from table*) This letter arrived by ship's messenger from Youghal three days ago.
THOMAS (*Takes letter*) Aye. From Mistress Greatrakes.
LIZZIE The Master did not even trouble to open it.
THOMAS He must have forgotten.

LIZZIE I know he has forgotten. I am not meddlesome, Thomas, I do not give scandal. But would you forget?

Pause.

THOMAS No. I would not.
LIZZIE I fear for him, Thomas — and I fear for the girl.
THOMAS I cannot think he means to harm her, Lizzie. He is an upright man.
LIZZIE I know that. But he may yet harm them both. In all the time I have been here, Thomas, I have not seen him more contented.
THOMAS Hooray for that, then — for he has been long enough discontented.
LIZZIE I do not begrudge him his good spirits but wonder at its source.
THOMAS She's a winsome lass, Lizzie — he enjoys her company — that is no sin, is it?
LIZZIE No. And I hope it may not become one.

MICHAEL enters. He wears a freshly laundered shirt, his hair is brushed for the first time. Reads aloud from playscript.

MICHAEL 'When Youth is ripe, and Age from time doth part,
The lifeless Trunk shall wed the Broken Heart.'

Closes book with a flourish. Pause.

I must find another play to read. Mr Everard says there are hundreds in the great world beyond, each with its own story. But how am I to find them?
THOMAS The Master has many books in his chamber. You should ask if he has playbooks there.
MICHAEL He has not. I looked when he was on the river with Angel yesterday and could find nought but holy books from wall to wall. I must find them,

Lizzie, for I begin to tire of the one story when there are so many to learn.

The double doors swing open with great gusto. GREATRAKES *stands at the other side.*

GREATRAKES My lords, ladies and gentlemen. May I present to the Court of Affane, Miss Angel Landy! (*Silence.* ANGEL *hangs back. We see her outline only*) Modest as well as beautiful. Come along, Angel, they won't bite!

ANGEL enters. Her appearance is radically transformed. The frayed dress, bare feet and unkempt hair are gone. She wears a bonnet, velvet cloak and buckled shoes and the overall impression is of a somewhat gaudy doll. ANGEL *is subdued and obviously ill at ease in her new vestments.* THOMAS, LIZZIE *and* MICHAEL *are, to varying degrees, shocked by her appearance, but must try to conceal this from* GREATRAKES.

Well, don't all speak at once! What do you think, Lizzie?
LIZZIE She is much altered.
GREATRAKES She most certainly is! You'd hardly recognise her, would you, Thomas?
THOMAS No, sir — she is entirely transformed.
GREATRAKES You have not seen the best of it yet! Take off the bonnet, Angel.

ANGEL self-consciously takes off the bonnet. We see that her hair has been got at and is now done up in ringlets or whatever.

Mark you that, Lizzie — I did not see its like at Whitehall Palace for my audience with the King.
LIZZIE I am sure you did not, Master.
GREATRAKES I note we have reduced Michael to silence, Angel

	— a not inconsiderable feat. What think you, boy?
MICHAEL	(*Pause. Glance at* LIZZIE) I think you look gallant, Angel.
GREATRAKES	Indeed she does, Michael. Thomas, take Angel's cloak and bonnet and show her to her place. (*Gestures to chair opposite head of table*) Here, if you will.
THOMAS	(*As he takes Angel's cloak and bonnet*) There, sir?
GREATRAKES	Yes, there. I will sit in my usual place. And you three along here. Are you ready to serve, Lizzie?
LIZZIE	Yes, Master.
GREATRAKES	Good. I thought to bring some port wine from the merchants for the occasion — I am sure God will not fault us for it.
MICHAEL	What *is* the occasion, Master?
GREATRAKES	Patience, Michael. All will be revealed. You may pour, Thomas.
THOMAS	Yes, sir.
ANGEL	(*Standing by chair at head of table*) Why must I sit here, sir?
GREATRAKES	Because you are our guest, Angel. You sit in the place of honour.
ANGEL	Is this not where Mistress Greatrakes would sit, sir?
GREATRAKES	Yes, it is. But Mistress Greatrakes is not here, is she? And so, as our guest, you may sit at the head of the table opposite me.
ANGEL	I do not wish to, sir.

Pause.

GREATRAKES	(*His patience straining again*) Do you not? Well you cannot always do as you wish, Angel. Sometimes we must do as we are ordained. So, if you please?
ANGEL	(*Defeated*) Yes, sir. (*She sits*)
GREATRAKES	Good.
THOMAS	(*Pouring wine*) Shall I pour for the child, sir?
GREATRAKES	That is no child, Thomas. That is a young lady. A tincture may bring some colour to her cheeks.

ANGEL I do not care to drink it, sir.
GREATRAKES Very well. Some cider then?
ANGEL I do not care for cider either, sir.
GREATRAKES I see. You are the very model of temperance. Bring Angel some water, Thomas.
THOMAS Yes, Master.
GREATRAKES Is everything in order, Lizzie?
LIZZIE (*A roast, vegetables etc. have been placed at the centre of the table*) It is, Master.
GREATRAKES Good. Then you may sit a moment before we serve. And if it is not too much trouble we may prevail upon Michael to do the same.
MICHAEL (*Patently aware of the girl's discomfort and the general tension*) May I be excused, Master?
GREATRAKES No, you may not. I requested your presence at my table — and now I will have it.
MICHAEL Please, Master. (*Looking at* LIZZIE) It is our mother's anniversary tomorrow. Lizzie and me thought to go to Salterbridge this evening to put flowers on her grave. Isn't that so, Lizzie?
LIZZIE (*Thinking fast*) Yes, Master. We did have a mind to.
GREATRAKES Then you may go when we have finished.
MICHAEL We cannot, Master. It would be dark before we got there.
GREATRAKES Then you may go tomorrow!
MICHAEL (*Through gritted teeth*) Very well, Master.

> MICHAEL *sits with others.* GREATRAKES *addresses them at the head of the table.*

GREATRAKES Thank you, Michael. (*Pause*) This evening, as you know, is Midsummer's Eve, the eve of the Summer Solstice, a night our pagan forefathers set aside to give thanks to their gods for the bounties those gods had bestowed upon them. On this Midsummer's Eve, I, too, would like to give thanks. Twelve years ago, Angel Landy emerged from the darkness of an English forest. All that she carried with her was the song that was on her lips, the same song she is now so cruelly prevented from singing. Some time past, Angel Landy came into our village and into our lives and brought that mystery with her. Two weeks ago she returned and this time she brought her pain. The pain of being silenced. (*Pause*) I have tried to heal that pain. I have tried to break that silence. I do not know if I can. (*Pause*) But we have had a surfeit of pain in this house. And so, this evening, if there is pain we cannot take away from her, there *is* something we can give to Angel. Something she has never known or never had. And that is, in the company of friends, in the company of family, the celebration of her day of birth. If there is much we cannot know, then let us celebrate what is known and give thanks that on this day Angel Landy came forth into the light. (*Pause*) Raise your glasses! To Angel! To her name day!

> GREATRAKES *drinks.* THOMAS *follows.* MICHAEL *and* LIZZIE *uncertain. They look at* ANGEL *who is obviously distressed.* GREATRAKES *looks at* MICHAEL *and* LIZZIE *who reluctantly drink.* ANGEL *begins to cry.*

                What ails you, girl?
ANGEL Nothing, sir.
GREATRAKES Then why are you crying?
ANGEL I do not know, sir.
GREATRAKES You are somewhat overcome, that is all. You will be fine presently. Come let us eat and be merry, we have had our fill of tears.
ANGEL I am not hungry, sir.
GREATRAKES But you must be! You did not eat since morning, Angel.
ANGEL And I do not wish to eat now!
GREATRAKES Angel, I remind you, this meal is in your honour.
LIZZIE Master, I think the child is tired from her

GREATRAKES exertions. Perhaps she should rest. I fail to see how donning the finest garments in Lismore can weary anybody.
ANGEL I did not ask for them, sir!
GREATRAKES I do not say you did! They were given willingly.
ANGEL (*On her feet*) But not received so! I do not want your fine clothes or buckled shoes. (*Rips buttons from dress and disrobes to petticoat*) I do not want your pretty ringlets and ribbons in my hair. (*These go also*) I do not want your name day, sir, for I have none! I only wish to sing!

ANGEL *runs from room. Silence.*

LIZZIE Shall I go after her, Master?
GREATRAKES (*Shouts*) Do as you see fit!

LIZZIE *exits. Silence.*

The horses are yet in harness to the carriage, Michael. When Lizzie is ready, you must go to Salterbridge as you planned. Put flowers on your mother's grave. And if you see your father, give him my respects.
MICHAEL I will, Master. He does often ask after you. (*Pause*) He remembers.
GREATRAKES Remembers what?
MICHAEL The curin', Master. What you did for me. He has not forgotten.
GREATRAKES I mean no disrespect, Michael. But I am heartily sorry that you and I ever met.
MICHAEL I am sure you must be, Master. But we did.

MICHAEL *exits. Silence.*

THOMAS The child is tired, is all. She will be well tomorrow.
GREATRAKES Yes. But she will not sing, will she?
THOMAS Who knows, sir? (*Pours wine for them both*) We finished the outhouses this evening.

GREATRAKES Yes. They look just like the old ones. Lizzie was right about that, too — you cannot burn memory.
THOMAS Speaking of memory, sir. Did you forget this (*Ruth's letter*)?
GREATRAKES No. I did not forget it.
THOMAS It is from Mistress Greatrakes, sir.
GREATRAKES I know who it is from.
THOMAS You should open it.
GREATRAKES For what purpose, Thomas? To read my children miss me? To read my wife swear undying love? But will not come home because her house is haunted with the spirits of those I betrayed? I need no letter to tell me as much.
THOMAS Sir, if the Mistress and the children will not come home, think you to go to them for a spell?
GREATRAKES What? To be judged by her there as she judged me here! And her father thrown in for good measure! A fine rest home that would be.
THOMAS She does not judge you, sir. No one does.
GREATRAKES No? Then you did not walk the streets of Lismore today, did you, Thomas? A mob — for that is what it was — a mob pursued me from shop to shop. Stood outside each window as I dressed the child, their number growing by the hour, as word spread the healer who would not heal was back in town. They said not one word between them or threatened us in any way but they judged me. Their palsied hands and their pock-marked faces judged and condemned me, Thomas. (*Pause*) And now the girl joins their ranks. (*Pause*) Ironic, isn't it? The voice I thought God's voice is silenced and I cannot make it sing. And she I thought God's messenger is here to turn the final screw. Well, let her judge me. Let them all judge and condemn me! But let them stand behind me in the queue. For though I am innocent of any crime, I have judged and condemned myself more than any have.
THOMAS God pity you, sir.

GREATRAKES Pity? Why should God pity when he may sneer, Thomas? In the darkness of these last months I thought, betimes, there *was* no God. That all was chance and happenstance, all life random and without pattern. (*Pause*) Would that we were so lucky! For what is worse than no God, Thomas, is an unheeding God — a God who has abandoned his suffering children to their fate. And what is worse than that, Thomas? A God who is no more than a cruel puppetmaster, dangling his puppets this way and that, simply to amuse himself and stave off boredom. One day a child can sing — the very proof of His existence, the next she is inexplicably dumbstruck. One day the healer can heal the afflicted, the next he is crippled too. Mister God could have cured us all, if He wanted to. I fancy now it is no more than a game and we must see which way He plays us.

LIZZIE *returns.*

How is the child?
LIZZIE She is resting, Master.
GREATRAKES Good. Perhaps she will wear her new dress tomorrow, Lizzie.
LIZZIE If she is made to.
GREATRAKES But you think she ought not be made to?
LIZZIE That is not for me to say, Master.
GREATRAKES I am asking you to say.
LIZZIE (*Putting on her own coat*) Michael is waiting, Master. He said we may go to Salterbridge.
GREATRAKES I thought only to make her happy, Lizzie.
LIZZIE You know what will make her happy.
GREATRAKES Yes. But that cannot be purchased at the draper's, can it?
LIZZIE It cannot be purchased at all, Master. (*Pause*) But it may be given away.
GREATRAKES How do you mean?

LIZZIE The girl will sing when the time comes, Master.
GREATRAKES (*Angry*) And what time will that be?
LIZZIE When you let her, Master.

Pause.

THOMAS I think you should go now, Lizzie.
GREATRAKES No! She will finish what she started. How do you mean, when I let her? I have been trying to restore the child every day since she came back here.
LIZZIE Your hands have, Master. But I believe your heart is ill-disposed to.
GREATRAKES Do you now? And since when are you privy to know how speaks my heart?
LIZZIE You bid me tell you what I think, Master. If you have no design to hear it —
GREATRAKES I have design to hear the truth! Not the tittle-tattle of my servants.
LIZZIE (*Going*) Then you will excuse me.
GREATRAKES No, I will not excuse you! Not until you explain yourself.
THOMAS Let her go, sir — it will serve no purpose.
GREATRAKES It will serve my purpose to understand what she means.
LIZZIE Then I will tell you, Master. And I will take the consequences. (*Pause*) I believe it is her voice no longer but the child herself enchants you now.
THOMAS That will do, Lizzie.
LIZZIE If you cure her she will leave but as long as you do not she is bound to you.
GREATRAKES I see. That is a subtle theorem — is it not, Thomas? Only it was you, not I, insisted she stay here, Lizzie. Or have you conveniently forgotten?
LIZZIE No, Master, I have not. But it were that she might sing again. Not to be dressed like some china poppet or fashioned in the image of something she is not and cannot be. You must let her go.
GREATRAKES Even if she do not sing?

LIZZIE She *will* sing, Master. But not for you.

Silence.

GREATRAKES I thank you for your candour, if nothing else, Lizzie.
LIZZIE There *is* something else.
GREATRAKES Why stop now?
LIZZIE If you heal her, the afflicted will return to the gates of this house within the hour. I think you know that is the price you will pay to set her free.
GREATRAKES Yes. And Mister God will have His sport all over again. (*Pause*) Well, not with me. I have been His dupe long enough. I will do as *I* please now. Burn this! (*Throws Angel's dress at* LIZZIE). Burn everything! The child may dress as she please but I will not let her go.
THOMAS She is not yours to keep, sir.
GREATRAKES No? Then what is mine to keep? My wife and children? My peace of mind? My faith? I have lost everything, Thomas.
THOMAS You have not yet lost your goodness, sir.
GREATRAKES Damn my goodness! Let my goodness rot in hell. I have paid too much for goodness and will be rid of it now. You speak more truth than you know, Lizzie Her spirit *does* move me, her mystery *does* enchant, her innocence *does* beguile.
LIZZIE You will destroy her, Master. You will *both* be destroyed.

Silence.

GREATRAKES How destroyed? Think you I want to bed her? Is that it, Lizzie? Is that what you think of your Master? (*Silence. Grabs her*) Answer me!
LIZZIE You must answer for yourself, Master.

GREATRAKES *hurls her violently to the floor.*

GREATRAKES No! (*Pause*) I may shed my goodness, but I am no monster!
LIZZIE You are a man, sir.
GREATRAKES *I am a cripple!* (*Pause*) *I am a cripple!* (*Silence*) Angel Landy pours balm upon my wounds. In her presence pain evaporates. Is that a crime? The girl may heal me, Lizzie. I cannot cure her but she may restore me. Not as God's puppet, not to serve the afflicted. But restored to my own self.
THOMAS You must save her to save yourself, sir.
GREATRAKES (*Looks intently at them*) Then we may both perish.

> GREATRAKES *exits. We hear a riff of the girl's voice 'front of house'. Its tone is troubled and agitated. Lights fade to end scene.*

Scene Three

The barn. Greatrakes' castle. Following day. MICHAEL *alone. He is pitching hay down through a trapdoor. After some time,* ANGEL *enters, now barefoot and wearing her own dress again. She watches* MICHAEL *briefly before approaching him.*

ANGEL Hello.
MICHAEL Holy Mother of God!
ANGEL I'm sorry. Did I frighten you?
MICHAEL (*Trying to recover with dignity*) You did not. There's nothing frightens me. (*Proffering a makeshift seat*) I see you're back in your own traps.
ANGEL Traps?
MICHAEL The dress, I mane.
ANGEL Oh. Yes.
MICHAEL 'Tis more your style too. And your hair — as wild as it is, at least it is your own.
ANGEL You said I looked gallant last night.
MICHAEL (*Coyly*) Did I? I was trying to cheer you only. For you looked terrible downcast in all your finery.
ANGEL I am better now.
MICHAEL You don't have to pretend, Angel.
ANGEL (*Smiles*) I won't then. (*Pause*) Salterbridge.
MICHAEL (*Surprised*) What about it?
ANGEL That's your home? You and Lizzie. I heard you say the name last night.
MICHAEL *Was* our home. Lizzie and me are in service here these five years and more.
ANGEL Salterbridge is still your home though. (*Pause*) It's a lovely name.
MICHAEL Do you think so?
ANGEL I do.
MICHAEL (*Pleased*) I never thought about it like that before. But now that you say it, I suppose it is.
ANGEL Will you tell me about it?
MICHAEL There's little to tell. Shur what is it, only a few *botháns* and a standpipe — you'd miss it entirely

if you sneezed on the road passin'. Though I'm lately for thinkin' this, Angel: the stories of a hole the like of your own place is as gallant as them you'd find anywhere. (*Pause*) Am I talkin' too much?

ANGEL I like listening to you.

MICHAEL (*Pause*) I like listenin' to you, too. Though you don't say much. Lizzie says she'll have me mouth stitched to shut me up but shur what harm is talkin'?

ANGEL None at all. Lizzie is very kind to me.

MICHAEL She's not the worst. Though a small bit mothery for my liking.

ANGEL Do you miss your mother?

MICHAEL Can you miss what you never had?

ANGEL I think so.

MICHAEL Lizzie and me were infants only when she died. My father it is remembers her for us, the way he's never done talkin' about her. Small blame to him, I suppose, for isn't that how you keep them alive — in your memory?

ANGEL Yes. If you have one.

Silence.

MICHAEL When the Master was speechifyin' at the table last night — was all he said true? About you comin' out of the forest and the like?

ANGEL Yes.

MICHAEL And that song on your lips, the same as you sang in the tent below?

ANGEL I cannot remember, but it is what Mr Everard says and he was there.

MICHAEL Well, isn't that a wonder! Who are you at all so?

ANGEL I do not know who I am. Angel Landy, I suppose. Mr Everard called me Landy after the forest I was found in.

MICHAEL And Angel because you are one, maybe.

ANGEL No. I am no Angel. I do not wish to be. I never

	cared to know what I was when I could sing. But it's different now. I miss to be singing, Michael.
MICHAEL	And why wouldn't you with a voice the like of it.
ANGEL	When I sang it did not matter who I was. That song was who I was. Mr Everard said we all have our place and purpose and that was mine. But it is gone now.
MICHAEL	It will come back, Angel.
ANGEL	Do you think so?
MICHAEL	As sure as Christmas.
ANGEL	Mr Greatrakes is not so sure.
MICHAEL	The Master is not sure of his name these days.
ANGEL	Then how will he heal me?
MICHAEL	I did not say *he* would.
ANGEL	Then who will?
MICHAEL	(*Shrugs without conviction*) You have to wait, Angel. As long as it takes. (*Pause*) I did.
ANGEL	For what?
MICHAEL	For a miracle.
ANGEL	I don't understand.

GREATRAKES *enters, unseen by* MICHAEL.

MICHAEL	All my life I have wondered about the world beyond my Master's fields and would I ever know its stories. I did often think to run away but, when the time came to go, I never did. So I waited. For something to happen. For something to make sense. (*Pause*) And then the playactors came. You and the playactors and the play. That was *my* miracle, Angel. You will have yours, too. But remember this: miracles is rooted in the clay, not the stars.

GREATRAKES *comes forward.*

GREATRAKES	Then we must seek them where we can find them.
MICHAEL	(*Separates from* ANGEL) Mr Greatrakes.

GREATRAKES   Wisely spoken, Michael — I underestimated you.
MICHAEL   It were only makin' up, sir — it were just for sport. (*Pause. Embarrassed*) The cot is below at the river field. If you'd fancy to go on the water with Angel.
GREATRAKES   No. Not this evening.
MICHAEL   The cows are for milking so. I'll go before they burst.

   MICHAEL *exits.*

GREATRAKES   How are you this evening?
ANGEL   I am well, sir. And you are angry with me.
GREATRAKES   I could not be angry with you.
ANGEL   You did not try to heal me today.
GREATRAKES   No. I did not.
ANGEL   Then will you try, now?
GREATRAKES   (*Pause*) No.
ANGEL   And tomorrow?
GREATRAKES   (*Pause*) No.
ANGEL   (*Panicking*) Then when, sir?
GREATRAKES   I will not try again. I have failed you, Angel.
ANGEL   No. You must not say that! I must be healed.
GREATRAKES   Then you must look elsewhere. I am sorry, Angel.

   Silence.

ANGEL   Very well, sir. I have to go now.
GREATRAKES   This may be for the best, Angel.
ANGEL   How can you say that, sir? How can you say that when my voice is all I possess? I am nothing without it.
GREATRAKES   Angel, we may learn that what we thought our gift was our greatest burden.
ANGEL   My voice was no burden. I am not you, sir. My voice *was* a gift. I have nothing without it.
GREATRAKES   You have other gifts in plenty.
ANGEL   And what are they, sir?
GREATRAKES   The gift to enchant? The gift to heal a broken

	heart?
ANGEL	If I had those gifts, it were my song alone accounted for them.
GREATRAKES	No. It were you, Angel. And you have not lost them. I am witness to as much.
ANGEL	(*Nervous of this*) I must go now, sir.
GREATRAKES	Please, do not be afraid.
ANGEL	I *am* afraid.
GREATRAKES	Of me?
ANGEL	Of what will become of me. I do not know who I am, Mr Greatrakes.
GREATRAKES	You are Angel Landy. Is that not enough?
ANGEL	When I could sing it were enough. But not anymore.
GREATRAKES	It is enough for me.
ANGEL	I want to go home, Mr Greatrakes.
GREATRAKES	Where is home, Angel?
ANGEL	I believed the playhouse were my home. I had a place there. But it is gone now.
GREATRAKES	There is a place for you here, Angel.
ANGEL	No.
GREATRAKES	Please. Hear me out. (*Pause*) Tomorrow at noon, a ship sails from Youghal for the port of Bristol. If you so choose, you may sail with it. I give you my word, I will not stand in your way. But I beg you to consider this: I could not heal you, Angel, but if you stay you may heal me.
ANGEL	I do not understand you, sir.
GREATRAKES	Something in my spirit has died and only you can resurrect it.
ANGEL	How can I, Mr Greatrakes?
GREATRAKES	I told you, you have many gifts. All I ask is your company. In return I will give you a home and a family.
ANGEL	Your family is gone, sir.
GREATRAKES	They will come back when I am healed.
ANGEL	I am not your healer. I came back here that you would heal me and you have not done so. Now you must heal yourself. I must go, sir.

GREATRAKES (*Restrains her*) No! Please, Angel. Do not leave me. (*His hands caress her face*) Only to behold you. That is all I desire.
ANGEL No! It is wrong, sir, it is wrong! I am frightened.
GREATRAKES I am frightened also. I am frightened of the dark, my Angel.
ANGEL Please, sir — let me go.
GREATRAKES (*His hands still cupping her face*) Only to behold you. That is all I ask.
ANGEL (*Crying*) No! You cannot! You must not!
GREATRAKES (*Crying also*) Tears become us now. (*He touches her tears with his finger, brushes a tear from his own face. Touches her lips with their tears*) My Angel's tears and mine conjoin, our separate grief unites.

He leans forward to kiss her. Stops just as he is about to. Recoils in horror.

Forgive me. Forgive me, my Angel.
ANGEL Mister Greatrakes —
GREATRAKES No more. No more. I am sorry, Angel. Leave me now. Leave me to the dark. (*Pause. Screams*) *Leave me!*

Silence. ANGEL *looks at him. Then rushes out. Lights fade.*

Scene Four

The forest at Affane. Dusk. A few days later. We open on the empty space. After a moment, MICHAEL *enters, bedraggled and exhausted. He collapses under a tree. Takes out a water pouch, drinks from it, pours some over his neck and head, wipes himself down with neckerchief. Sits in silence a moment.* LIZZIE *enters.*

LIZZIE (*Joining* MICHAEL) Well?
MICHAEL Divil the sign of her, Lizzie. And you?
LIZZIE She has not come back. But you must, Michael.
MICHAEL No.
LIZZIE Michael, it is four days today.
MICHAEL If it be four days and forty, it makes no odds to me. I must wait for her.
LIZZIE She is not here, Michael.
MICHAEL She *is*. I know she is.
LIZZIE The woodsmen have scoured every inch of the forest — you have done as much yourself. She is not here.
MICHAEL She is here. I know it, Lizzie. She will show when she has a mind to.
LIZZIE And what of my mind that is near demented with worry?
MICHAEL You have no call for worryin'. I am well, Lizzie. I will come home when Angel does.
LIZZIE Angel is not coming home, Michael. (*Pause*) There is news.

Pause. MICHAEL *looks at her.*

Osborne's men searched the river fields today. They found Angel's dress at the water's edge. The boatmen are dragging the river, Michael.

Silence.

MICHAEL No! (*Pause*) No. They will drag in vain. Angel is

LIZZIE   not in the water. She would not do such a thing.
MICHAEL   How do you know what she would do? She is not well, Michael.
LIZZIE   No. But she will be. She will sing again and then she will be well. (*Pause*) I know she is near, Lizzie. I *must* wait for her.

> *Pause.* LIZZIE *takes out cloth bundle from under her jacket, unwraps it and takes out some food.*

LIZZIE   Then you will eat, at least.
MICHAEL   I am not hungry.
LIZZIE   You will need your strength, Michael — whatever unfolds. (*He takes food and eats*)
MICHAEL   How fares the Master?
LIZZIE   As you would imagine. He has not left his room these four days. Thomas says he neither eats nor sleeps but gives day and night in silence at his casement.
MICHAEL   It were not his fault. He tried to save her, didn't he, Lizzie?
LIZZIE   Yes. I believe he did. But Angel could not save *him*.

> GREATRAKES *enters. He carries Angel's dress. Joins* MICHAEL *and* LIZZIE.

GREATRAKES   And so . . . All is darkness now, Michael.
MICHAEL   There is light yet in the sky, Master.
GREATRAKES   But not for long. 'I'm afeard of nothin', sir — except the dark!' That's what he told me, Lizzie. All those years ago. Was this what we both waited for, Michael? Is it here, now? (*Pause*) They brought me her dress. Why did they bring it to me? Why did they bring it to *me*, Lizzie?
LIZZIE   I do not know, Master.
GREATRAKES   (*Suspends dress from the branch of a tree*) If you love her, you must let her go, you said. And I did, Lizzie. I let her go, did I not?

LIZZIE   Yes, Master, you did.
GREATRAKES   Such a beautiful child. I warrant she will not look so beautiful when the river gives her up.
MICHAEL   The river does not have her to give up, Master. Angel Landy is not dead.
GREATRAKES   Then where is she?
MICHAEL   She is looking for her song.
GREATRAKES   Greatrakes stole her song.
MICHAEL   And Angel will find it again.
GREATRAKES   No. It is gone. And the child with it. Nothing left but a soiled garment. I tried to burn that too, Lizzie. But I could not. You cannot burn memory.
MICHAEL   I will keep it for her. For when she comes back.
GREATRAKES   I fear your faith will not be rewarded, Michael.
LIZZIE   (As GREATRAKES *moves away*) Master?

GREATRAKES *stops.*

Master, would you pray with us?
GREATRAKES   Pray? For what?
LIZZIE   For Angel? For her deliverance — dead or alive.
GREATRAKES   And to whom, Lizzie? To whom shall we pray for anyone's deliverance now? To Mister God in the dark skies above? (*Pause*) Mister God will not delude me again. I have done with prayer, Lizzie — the air of liberation is sweet now and I will not be shackled again. I have murdered an innocent child, I have murdered innocence itself. I can fall no further — Mr Greatrakes is free at last.

THOMAS *and* RUTH *enter.*

RUTH   And what will he do with his freedom? Use it well, Valentine — you have paid dearly for it.
GREATRAKES   (*Shocked to see her*) Ruth? Is it Ruth?
RUTH   You know it is. (*Pause*) Will no one bid me welcome?
LIZZIE   We have missed you, Ma'am.
RUTH   And I have missed you, Lizzie. (*Looking at* GREATRAKES) All of you.

GREATRAKES I am glad to see you, Ruth.
RUTH Are you?
GREATRAKES Where are the children?
RUTH They are at the house. I have brought them home, Valentine. We will learn to live with our ghosts.
GREATRAKES Then you must add another to their number.
RUTH I have heard about the child.
THOMAS I took liberty to acquaint the Mistress, sir. I thought it best.
GREATRAKES Yes. You must all do what you think best. (*Pause*) What news from the river?
THOMAS None, sir. The boatmen have gone home and will return at first light.
RUTH I am sorry, Valentine.
GREATRAKES Yes. So am I, Ruth. For everything.
RUTH The child may yet be found.
GREATRAKES There are no more miracles, Ruth. Angel Landy has found her peace. I may find mine, too, before this night is out.
RUTH Where? At the bottom of the Blackwater? Hanging from a tree in the dead of night? Did I bring our children home to that?
GREATRAKES They must leave again. And you with them. I have destroyed enough, Ruth! Let my children be spared.
RUTH You decide, Valentine. If you perish, we will perish with you. All of us.
GREATRAKES No! Please, Ruth, leave me be. I must have my peace now.
RUTH (*Takes his head in her hands*) I will give you peace. Sleep in my arms tonight, Valentine. Hold me close. Heartbeat to heartbeat. Love to love. (*Pause*) Innocence regained.
GREATRAKES (*Breaking away*) No! It is too late! I have murdered innocence, Ruth. Innocence lies in a wet grave and will never ever be regained!

> *Silence. The blind man,* MARTIN REILLY, *enters the forest, some distance away. Approaches tentatively, a rough stick guiding his path.*

MARTIN Mr Greatrakes? Mr Greatrakes? Is it you, sir?

Silence.

Please. I heard voices. Is it you, Mr Greatrakes?

Silence.

RUTH (*Looking at* GREATRAKES) You have found who you seek.
MARTIN (*Falling to his knees*) Jesus be praised! Sweet Jesus be praised!
GREATRAKES What do you want of me?
MARTIN You know what I want, sir.
GREATRAKES I have nothing to give.
MARTIN Please, sir. I have travelled far.
GREATRAKES Then you have travelled in vain.
MARTIN No, sir. But in hope. And in faith, sir. Three days and three nights I have journeyed, the kindness of strangers and the hand of God guiding my path.
GREATRAKES Then God sports with you, too, my friend — as is His wont.
MARTIN Please, Mr Greatrakes. I must see my child. I have been too long in darkness. I believe, Mr Greatrakes. I believe.
GREATRAKES What? In Holy God's infinite mercy!
MARTIN No, sir. In *you*. I believe in you.
GREATRAKES No one believes in me. We are joined in darkness now, my friend. Eternal darkness.
MARTIN Please, sir —
GREATRAKES Bring him to the house, Michael. Give him food and shelter. And, tomorrow, see that he is returned safely to his wife and child.
MARTIN No, sir. My wife does not know where I am. I will not go back until I can see. I have been blind since birth, Mr Greatrakes. What I never had did never trouble me until I met you. You gave me hope, sir. You will not take it away from me now.

GREATRAKES You have my instructions, Michael.
MICHAEL I have, Master. But I will not heed them.
GREATRAKES Thomas? Will you do as I bid?
THOMAS You taught me the meaning of loyalty a long time ago, sir. I hope you have counted me loyal and I will not desert you now. (*Pause*) So the answer is no — I will not do as you bid.
GREATRAKES I see it is not just God who sports with me now. (*Pause*) Lizzie? Will you deny him shelter?
LIZZIE It is not shelter he seeks, Master.
GREATRAKES I do not *have* what he seeks!
LIZZIE I believe you do, Master. We all do.

>GREATRAKES *takes them in, one by one, his eyes finally resting on* RUTH.

RUTH You are a good man, Valentine. I have never doubted it. I never will.

>*Silence.* GREATRAKES *looks at her, at his hands, at the blind man kneeling before him.* GREATRAKES *approaches him and places his hands on the man's eyes, the gesture this time made in silence. After a moment, the young man's eyelids begin to flicker and it gradually and very quietly becomes apparent that his sight has been restored. He looks into Greatrakes' eyes, looks at the others, then at the forest which surrounds him and finally back to* GREATRAKES, *tears now streaming from his eyes.*

GREATRAKES You have your peace now.
MARTIN Thank you, sir. Thank you.
GREATRAKES (*To* THOMAS) Bring him to the house. See that he is looked after.
THOMAS Yes, sir.

>THOMAS *and* MARTIN *exit.* LIZZIE *gestures to* MICHAEL *that they should leave also.*

MICHAEL I must wait for Angel.
LIZZIE She will come when she is ready. You were right, Michael. The river did not claim her. (*Looking at* GREATRAKES) She *is* here.

LIZZIE *and* MICHAEL *exit.*

RUTH The children await you. What shall I tell them?

Silence.

GREATRAKES Tell them their father has also come home. Tell them he has accepted his destiny. (*Pause*) It is as you said. We must sacrifice ourselves to it. (*He looks at Angel's dress.* RUTH *looks at it also*) But at what price, Ruth? At what price?

> RUTH *exits.* GREATRAKES *alone. He crosses to Angel's dress, picks it up — tentatively, delicately, as though it might still contain the child's lifeless body.* GREATRAKES, *desolate, beholds it in wonder, running its thin fabric through the fingers of his hands. Then presses it to his face, agonisingly inhaling its scent. Clings to the dress, falls to his knees, collapsing in tears on the forest floor. Pause.*
>
> *Then we hear the voice of Angel Landy in the distance. Gradually coming closer until* ANGEL *herself appears, naked, dishevelled and bleeding. She enters upstage and is seen as through a mist.* GREATRAKES *gradually becomes aware of her voice. He does not 'see' the child — her voice is inside his head.* ANGEL *continues singing, comes further downstage as* GREATRAKES *again beholds the dress, finally holding it aloft in a last ecstatic gesture as* ANGEL *sings on and the lights fade to black.*